MW00790641

BROKEN SHIELD

BOBBI & TIM HAYS -

YOU'RE NEVER ALONE WHEN YOU'RE
READING A BOOK.

I HOPE THAT BROKEN SHIELD
WILL BE A GREAT COMPANION.

All the best!

Ray C. Morrow

BROKEN SHIELD

Bobbi + Tim Hays

YOU'RE NEVER ALONE WHEN YOU'RE
READING A BOOK.
I HOPE THAT BROKEN SHIELD
WILL BE A GREAT COMPANION.

BROKEN SHIELD

AN FBI UNDERCOVER AGENT'S PERSONAL PERSPECTIVE

RAY A. MORROW
WITH
LINDSAY PRESTON

Distributed by Bublish, Inc.

Paperback ISBN: 978-1-64704-138-0
Hardback ISBN: 978-1-64704-140-3
eBook ISBN: 978-1-64704-139-7

This book is dedicated to my beloved father, Clarence Austin Morrow, who sadly passed away at the young age of 51. This is for you dad, as you always demanded excellence from me when I was simply satisfied with mediocrity. I am who I am today because of you.

PREFACE

This is the story of my two great loves. One is my wife (and children). The other, which often took priority, is my love affair with the FBI. As far back as I can remember, I wanted to be an FBI Special Agent. From the time I was a child, I was enthralled with J. Edgar Hoover and the Federal Bureau of Investigation. During the 1960s, he was one of the most powerful men in the United States. He was always meticulously dressed and fastidious when it came to following the law. He held the key to a just and right world. I would watch him on our small black and white television, and I knew that I wanted to be a part of the most exceptional investigative organization in the world.

The path to becoming a Special Agent is never straight, nor is it the same for everyone. But those who make it through Quantico do so out of passion. But it doesn't take long for a young agent to learn that "you can love the FBI, but it can't love you back." Even so, I sacrificed my family to protect my investigations and my FBI family. I often struggled with the demands of my two worlds and realized I had to do whatever it took to maintain my family while also maintaining control of my career and future. I had no idea at the time how difficult a challenge I was about to undertake. It looked so effortless on television and in the movies.

I was not prepared for the case that would change the trajectory of both my career and family. I had only been in the Bureau for two years when a lead undercover position became available in Cleveland, Ohio. To say I was inexperienced would be an understatement; I hadn't even assisted on an undercover case. But I had just read Joe Pistone's book, DONNIE BRASCO, and had the undercover itch. I knew that this was the direction I wanted my career to go, and I was willing to do whatever it took to get it there. Even with all my enthusiasm and training, I could never prepare myself for what lay ahead. But part of me thought, 'Hey, I just read Donnie Brasco, I should be able to pull this off.'

For two years, I served as the Primary Undercover Agent on one of the most significant police corruption investigations in history. During that time, I became engrossed in a world so vastly different from my own that I had no choice but to detach. When I signed on, I never realized what an emotional toll the investigation would have on my life. Most people, even FBI agents, don't understand the depths you must dive into becoming someone else. The waters get murky and dark, and only the strong can resurface after sinking so deep.

My FBI undercover investigation targeted the Cleveland, Ohio Police Department. SHIRON, as the case was named, began in May 1989 and ended in May 1991. During my undercover operation, I made over 1,000 audio body recordings, over 500 video and telephone recordings of conversations with corrupt police officers involved in numerous criminal activities such as dealing in stolen property, bookmaking operations, narcotics, assault, and battery, and money laundering.

The investigation concluded with the indictments of forty-seven individuals, thirty of whom were police officers. Three trials followed immediately after that, and all were completed by 1992. I was incredibly proud of what we (the Cleveland FBI Field Office and United States Attorney's Office in the Northern District of Ohio) had accomplished in our undercover operation.

I hope this story depicts the sacrifices made by the members of the FBI and their families in order to keep the world a safe and just place to live.

CHAPTER

April 21, 1966

"I am looking for information about a fugitive named Larry Drake," Inspector Lewis Erskine said, his voice commanding.

"Why you lookin' for him?" the man said, taking a drag of his cigarette.

"He's an escaped prisoner who murdered three law enforcement officers in cold blood during his escape, and one of those officers just happened to be one of my closest friends," the Inspector replied.

I leaned in closer towards the little black and white television. I was just eleven years old with my face inches from the tube. My chubby fingers grasped the long strands of our tan shag carpet. Inspector Erskine's eyelids dropped, and a fierce look crossed his handsome face. I twisted my face to try to match the Inspector's signature look. I was captivated. The "The FBI" starring Efrem Zimbalist Jr. aired for the first time in 1965, and since then, I never missed a weekly episode. I could not get enough of the Agents and their cases. "The FBI" followed Inspector Lewis Erskine's investigations very carefully, and I was right there, hanging onto his coattails.

I was fascinated by his dapper and sophisticated dress and appearance. I had never seen anyone quite as refined as Erskine. And I certainly had never met anyone busy saving the world. On top of the mystery and adventure, I loved the structure and guidance the show depicted. I became enthralled with those that strictly adhered to and upheld the laws, regulations, policies, and procedures. I was already in love with the FBI.

I lived in Hopewell Township in western Pennsylvania, a classic blue-collar mid-America town. There wasn't much to do or much around other than the steel mills, factories, and hills. My father worked at the J&L Steel mill and my mother at the Phoenix Glass factory. They were hard-working people that couldn't even imagine leaving their hometown. Western PA was filled with hard-working, dedicated blue-collar workers, who took great pride in what they did for a living. This work ethic and pride were instilled in all of us, especially some of my closest friends from junior high and high school. Friends like Ed Wilamowski, Danny Raines, Joe Durinsky, Bob Rosati, Bill Sosko, Jeff Hineman, Ed Burak, Gary Ciccone, Tony Dorsett, and others. All of my friends and I competed in high school athletics. Most of us played high school football and baseball. There wasn't much else to do at the time, and this is what was expected of boys.

Joining the FBI was a dream that most people from our small town would never consider pursuing. That was for big-city folk. Most of the residents of Hopewell ended up working in the steel mills or other factory jobs that were in abundance. The mills offered a great way to make a living just like our fathers and their fathers before them. But I knew that it was not for me. I *had* to be an FBI Special Agent.

My father was on the same page as me, at least as it came to my future in a factory. Although he did the backbreaking work and knew it put plenty of food on the table, he wanted more for me. He was a huge proponent of my getting a college education and was tough on me when it came to my studies and, most importantly, my grades. There was no way I was not going to college on his watch. But we didn't necessarily see eye to eye on what my future had to hold.

"I'm gonna be an FBI agent," I announced as my father walked into the living room.

My father gulped his coffee and wiped his mouth. "Son, you ain't going to do no such thing. You are going to be a pharmacist, end of story."

I wasn't even sure what a pharmacist did at the time, but I knew that was not what I wanted to do. But I also knew better than to argue with my dad. He was a strict disciplinarian, and his word was gospel. His personality made him seem far larger than his slight 5'9" frame. His dream for me to receive a college education and have a good white-collar job, contradictory to his upbringing. He had dropped out of school at 14 to help support his mother, father, and six siblings. He later joined the Navy, where he learned numerous trades such as carpentry, auto mechanics, electrical wiring. He could fix any piece of machinery or a small appliance.

My mom, on the other hand, was a typical Italian Catholic mother. She was dedicated to her family. She loved to cook, clean, socialize, and play cards with family and friends. While she couldn't imagine me leaving Hopewell, because no one ever did, she wanted me to have the world. "You go on believing you can do anything, Ray," she would say, her smile sincere.

♥ ♥ ♥

1968

My mother licked her hand and wiped it across my brown hair, tapping down the straggling strands of my colic. "You look so handsome, Ray," my mother said as she stepped back to look at me in my suit and bow tie.

I looked at myself in the mirror and gave each side of my plaid bowtie a tight tug. I smoothed down my blonde hair. I was pretty proud of my appearance, a dapper man like Inspector Erskine, I thought to myself.

"We need to get to church now," my father hollered from the other room.

"I'm ready," I yelled back. I straightened my blue jacket and smiled at my mom.

"You will do great," she said.

We got in our a 1966 Chevy Impala and headed down Brodhead Road towards Center Township. It took 15 minutes for us to arrive at St. Francis Cabrini Church in Center Township. St. Francis was the only catholic church in Center Township. Our Lady of Fatima was the Catholic Church in Hopewell, but my mother and father were good friends with Father O'Connell at St. Francis Cabrini, so that's where we attended mass every Sunday. St Francis Cabrini was a simple building with an elementary school and social hall. As we pulled up into the parking lot, I saw all of my friends and their families gathered outside. It was my Confirmation day.

4

I had attended church and catechism classes every week from the time I was five. My mom's side of the family was a strict Italian Catholic family, and my Confirmation was a big deal. We greeted everyone and then quickly entered the chapel and found seats as close as we could. I slid into the sixth row; first, my entire family sat with the rest of the families towards the back of the church.

I felt the nerves rise in my belly, and I fiddled in my seat.

When my name was called, I humbly approached the bishop. I was nervous. I glanced at my mother; she was beaming, her hands clutching her rosary. I moved forward in the line, my head slightly bowed as I waited for my turn. Finally, it was my turn. I stood in front of Bishop John Joseph Wright. He gave me a warm smile and then crossed my forehead with his cross.

"Ray Anthony Joseph Morrow, may you be sealed with the gift of the Holy Spirit."

"Amen," I replied.

"Peace be with you," he said.

I bowed my head in respect and made my way back to my seat for the Priest to conclude Mass. After Mass, my mother and father came up to the altar to say a few words to me.

"Ray, your mother, and I are so proud. We want you to keep the values of the church in your heart. And remember that the right decision is often the hardest one to make, but by doing do so, you are building character," my dad said, his voice full of emotion.

My dad reached into his pocket and pulled out a small box. He opened it, and my mom reached in and pulled out a medallion, the face Jesus carved in the center.

"May you continue to walk in the light of Jesus," my mother said, kissing the medallion and hanging it around my neck. "I love you, Raymond."

♥ ♥ ♥

I was playing shortstop and pitcher on my little league baseball team, had lots of friends, was doing well in school, and active in my church. But despite my full life, the mystique of the FBI was always with me. I wouldn't say I was obsessed, but I was probably close to it.

"Ray, are you ready?" my father called from downstairs.

"I am," I said excitedly.

I skipped down the steps in my white and red little league uniform. I was ready for the first game of the season.

"I need to stop at the Township building before the game. We can walk over to the field right after," my dad said. My dad had to make his quarterly tax payment, a task he did in person.

The Hopewell Township Building was a 10-minute drive from my house. It was located in the town square. The baseball fields were behind the Hopewell Junior High School next door to the Township Building. And across the road was a snow cone stand that made the best snow cones. I was looking forward to my cherry snow cone after my game today!

When we arrived, I went in with my father, but he asked me to wait in the lobby area while he went into one of the offices. As I waited, I noticed a group of Hopewell Police officers gathered around a gentleman who was leading the conversation. This gentleman was well dressed in a dark blue suit and red tie, dark-colored fedora hat, and his shoes were shined. His chiseled jaw and broad shoulders reminded me of Inspector Erskine. And he had the complete attention of the Officers. I stood in awe of the gentleman.

My eyes adhered to the man like they did to the television when watching THE F.B.I. I knew there had to be something special about him. We didn't see a lot of suits in Hopewell, and even when we did, they weren't like the one this man was wearing. I wasn't sure how much time had passed until my father emerged from the office.

My father gave a wave towards the group of police officers. My heart stopped, did my dad know the well-dressed man? The excitement started brewing in the back of my throat but quickly dissipated as one of the cops headed towards my father and me.

"How ya' doing, Clancy?" the cop asked my dad.

"I'm good, Mitch. This is my boy, Ray," my dad tells the cop.

"Nice to meet you, Ray," the cop says, sticking out his hand.

"Nice to meet you, too," I replied.

My father and the cop began shooting the breeze. I waited quietly for the conversation to end. I had made up my mind that I was going to ask Officer Mitch about the man. I needed to know!

"Nice to see you, Clancy," the cop said, getting ready to walk away.

"Excuse me, Officer Mitch," I said, my voice quiet. My dad had his stink eye glued to me as soon as the first word left my mouth.

"Yes, Ray?" the cop replied.

"Who was the man in the suit you were speaking to?" I asked, my eyes low.

"The man with the hat?"

I nodded.

"He is an FBI Agent from the Pittsburgh FBI Field Office," he said.

My eyes widened, and a smile crossed my face. I had just seen the real-life Inspector Erskine, and I knew right then that I was absolutely going to be an FBI agent! The excitement that filled within me was something I had never experienced before. It was like seeing Superman up close and personal. I wanted so badly to go over and introduce myself to the FBI Agent, but I knew my father would have none of it, and I needed to get to the baseball field to get ready for my game.

♥ ♥ ♥

1970

"You're home! You're home!" my 8-year-old sister, Violet, squealed from down the hall.

I hopped off my bed and sprinted to the back door. "Dad!"

We both ran towards him, full speed ahead. My mom jumped in front of us, blocking our furious hugs.

"Gentle with your father. He is still frail," mom said, her tone calm.

"I'm okay, Margaret. Hugs won't hurt me," my father said.

"Clancy, you heard what the doctors said."

My father opened his arms wide. Violet and I slowly

approached our father and simultaneously hugged him. He had spent the week in the hospital from a back injury at work. He was placed in traction while in the hospital. Spinal traction was a form of decompression therapy that relieves pressure on the spine. It can be performed manually or mechanically but always by medical professionals. Spinal traction is used to treat herniated discs, sciatica, degenerative disc disease, pinched nerves, and many other back conditions.

My mom and I helped my father to the couch. "Can I get you anything, Clancy?" my mom asked.

"I'm just going to take a little rest here on the couch," he said. This was the first time in my life that I saw my father look weak and frail. He could barely hold himself up. My father laid on the couch and fell asleep. He had always been the most strong-willed and strong-minded person I had known; thus, his current condition was very unsettling to me. I sat on the floor in front of the couch and watched him sleep. After a half-hour or so, my mom sent me to my room to play with Violet.

Even though there was an eight-year age difference between Violet and me, we got along well. I was happy to play games with her, often letting her win. We were in the middle of a game of Candyland when I heard the bathroom door shut. I figured my dad was awake. I headed out to the living room. I was anxious to spend some time with him. I walked into the hallway just in time to see my father stumble out of the bathroom.

"You okay, dad?" I asked.

He fumbled forward. I reached out and grabbed him

before he hit the floor. As I lowered my dad to the ground, I screamed, "MOM!"

The bathroom floor was covered in blood. I couldn't tell where the blood had come from. My mom ran into the room, and she screamed, "Call an ambulance!"

The ambulance arrived and rushed my father to the hospital. My father had a bleeding ulcer. Once at the hospital, after they were able to get him stabilized, they operated and removed 2/3 of his stomach. After that, his health began to deteriorate. My father was never the same.

One year later, my father had open-heart surgery; this was a difficult time for all of us. My dad was only 43 years old at the time, and due to the operation was forced to take a disability retirement from J&L Steel. The doctors had told us that his demeanor might change, and it did. He went from being an outgoing, personable individual to a more introspective and quieter individual who was, at times, quick to anger. It was a hard adjustment for all of us, especially for my father.

♥ ♥ ♥

1972

As my desire and passion to become an FBI Special Agent continued to grow throughout my high school years, I was determined that I was going to college to get a degree in law enforcement. However, my father's desire for me to go on to college and become a pharmacist was steadfast. There were numerous conversations between my father and me regarding this, and I never won any of those conversations.

"Dad, I really want to be an FBI agent," I explained calmly.

"Son, life is not one of your silly television shows. The FBI is a pipe dream. You will be a pharmacist. It is a great profession to support a family, plus it is a vital job for the community. Look at Mr. Reynolds at Crest Cut Rate Drugstore. That is what you want to be!"

That was the last thing in the world I wanted to be, but I also didn't want to upset my father. Thus, I never argued, but from time to time would remind him of my desires, especially as I entered my senior year in high school, and it came time to apply to colleges.

Finally, I said to myself I have got to get this situation under control and convince my father that law enforcement was my career choice. Time was running out, and applications for college admittance would soon be upon us. For days I practiced, researched, and rehearsed what I was going to say to convince my father. I went to the library for days and researched the ins and outs of the FBI. I put together a solid pitch for my father. I certainly did not want to disappoint him as I was going to be the first in his family to go to college. He was incredibly proud of that, and I wanted him to be proud of what I was choosing to do. After several days of preparation, I was ready.

I hemmed and hawed for days on the best time to approach my dad with my pitch. I had to get him when he was in a good mood, but I wanted to catch him off guard and unprepared. I wanted him to listen to me. I just wanted an opportunity to get it all out. Hell, I had been working on this for days. The least he could do was listen.

I thought the best time for the attack would be right after

dinner when he sat down to read the paper and watch the news on TV. I figured his mind would be elsewhere, and maybe just maybe I could slip this by him.

"How was your day, Violet?" my dad asked.

"It was good. I ate lunch with my friend Sarah, and then we played hopscotch at recess," Violet said, taking a bite of spaghetti.

"How about you, Ray?" he asked.

"Good. Got an A on my English test," I said.

"That's my boy," he said, taking a bite of the meatball. "Dinner is wonderful as usual, Margaret."

My mom smiled. She was a fantastic cook and made the best Italian dinners. We had dinner as a family almost every day. After dinner, we would all go our separate ways. My dad, like usual, headed to his favorite chair to read the paper and watch the news. I walked to my room to gain my composure.

I took a deep breath, walked out of my bedroom down the hall to the living room where my dad was sitting. I was nervous as hell but kept saying to myself calm down, relax; you can do this. This is your future, not his. But in a way, I knew it was my father's future as well. He worked so hard to give me everything he could, and now it was my turn to repay him. To make him proud of me. And I knew that if I explained how much I wanted to be an FBI agent if I could sell that to him, he would agree with me. At least that's what I thought. Or should I say hope? My mother had joined him in the living room and was seated on the couch.

"Dad, we need to talk."

My father folded down the top of his newspaper, peered over the now bent newspaper, and was looking right at me.

"Dad, I know you want me to go to school to be a Pharmacist, but have you seen any of my science grades. I'd never make it. Besides I want to go to school for law enforcement, I want to be an FBI agent. That's my dream. That is what I am most passionate about."

My mother started to cry. She was extremely emotional and would cry at the drop of a hat. This time I think she was crying because she thought my father and I were about to have one big hullabaloo. I was hoping that her crying just might help.

"Well, you know, a Pharmacist is a very admirable career," he said, his eyes peering over his paper. I was about to jump in and go further with my plea, I was loaded for bear filled with facts about a career in the FBI, but my father continued, but, if you love what you do, you'll never have to work a day in your life." He flipped his newspaper back up and went back to reading.

What the hell just happened, I thought to myself as I walked back to my room. I had plenty more to say, all that research and preparing down the drain. But I guess it didn't matter. He just said I could pursue my dreams. I was ecstatic, as I walked into my bedroom, I looked in the mirror and said, "Ray Morrow, FBI, you're under arrest."

CHAPTER

September 1973

I was accepted at Penn State University and enrolled in their Law Enforcement and Corrections program. I walked onto campus for the first time at the Penn State Beaver Campus on September 04, 1973. The campus was only 15 miles from my home. I commuted to school and lived at home, as did many of my high school friends and classmates. The first year at PSB felt more like the 13th year at high school, which made it a smooth transition.

I joined the Penn State Beaver baseball team, and several of my teammates from high school were also on the team. I was the starting right fielder for the Penn State Beaver Baseball team for both my freshman and sophomore years. It was a great way to start college life.

My first class was Tuesday at 9 am. I was so excited to take my first class. It was Sociology, I walked into the small lecture room 20 minutes early, butterflies in my stomach. I took a seat in the front row. I had waited my entire life to head down this path. I wasn't going to miss a thing. Thirty seconds before the bell rang, a muscular, athletic-looking young man sat down next to me. He had curly blonde hair neatly coiffed and stuck his hand out to me. "I'm Robert Shuster. But you can call me Shoo."

"Shoe?"

"Yep. And what should I call you?" he asked.

"Ray. Ray Morrow."

Shoo and I became the best of friends. We were in the same law enforcement program at school and were in all the same classes throughout our four years. We spent our last two years at Penn State University's main campus as roommates. This was the first time I had ever met someone with the same intense interest in law enforcement as myself. And he was instrumental in helping me to graduate on time. It turned out that Shoo was a diligent student. And he was certainly more dedicated to studying than I was, and he insisted that I study with him, and I usually acquiesced as I did not want him to use his Black Belt karate skills on me.

During my four years at Penn State, I had the opportunity to do two Internships. I did my first internship with Shoo at the Beaver County Narcotics Bureau. I flew solo on my second internship at the Ellwood City, PA Police Department. It was during these internships that I realized this was my calling. This is what I was meant to do.

December 1976

It was a blustery cold day in December when Shoo and I reported to the first day of our internship at the Beaver

County Narcotics Bureau. The Beaver County Courthouse was close to our homes but approximately 175 miles from Penn State Main Campus. Shoo and I were both staying at our parent's homes while we completed our internship. I left my parent's house early to fight the snow and ensure I was at our first assignment on time. Shoo lived a little closer but arrived at about the same time I did. My drive took about twenty minutes as I traveled the Beaver County Expressway to the Beaver Exit. We made it on time. Leaving a trail of snowy footsteps, we headed toward the front desk to check-in.

"Can I help you?" the receptionist asked.

Neither of us spoke. Be it the cold or the nerves, we were frozen.

"Can I help you?" she asked again.

I shook off my nerves and the last bit of snow and said, "I am Ray Morrow, and this is Shoo, Robert Shuster. We are interns from Penn State University."

"Welcome, Mr. Morrow and Mr. Schuster. Detective Bob Karwoski is expecting you. Head down this hallway, and he will be in the back room. You won't miss him," she said with a smile.

She was right. There was no missing Bob Karwoski. At 6'3" and 245 pounds, he was larger than life. A mop of thick black hair topped his rugged face. He was soft-spoken but still commanded a room. When Bob spoke, everyone listened. It was apparent Bob loved fighting bad guys.

The Beaver County Narcotics Bureau was comprised of three detectives and a supervisor. Besides the three detectives, there were two clerical workers. Shoo and I were assigned to work directly with the detectives addressing all narcotics violations. Bob made detective work look effortless. After a week on the job I decided that I no longer wanted to be like Inspector Erskine, I wanted to be like Bob Karwoski.

We worked long hours and late nights in areas of Beaver County that I had never seen before. Areas that I had been told that 'good people' just don't go; areas that were well known for fights, drugs, and muggings. I saw a different part of life, something I never knew existed during the hours I had never been awake to see. And no matter how hard or late we worked the night before, we were expected in the office bright and early the next morning. I unequivocally loved it. I was having the time of my life and learning what it took to work in law enforcement. Long hours, nights, weekends, no matter what, you had to be ready, prepared, and respond appropriately. Former United States Senator, Ms. Barbara Boxer once stated; "Law enforcement officers are never off duty. They are dedicated public servants who are sworn to protect public safety at any time and place that peace is threatened. They need all the help they can get."

I sat on stakeouts and worked mobile surveillances. I found neither of those to be as exciting as I saw on television. My internship was a real learning experience on how to develop an investigation to bring it to its rightful conclusion. I watched Bob interview witnesses, work informants, set up, and make drug buys and do the paperwork. Bob was artistic in how he went about his business.

"If it's not documented, it never happened," Bob would say. "Always document everything accurately and precisely, for everyone's sake. You hold a lot of power with your badge, and if you don't use that power correctly, your screwed.

Always remember that there are twelve people watching everything you do." Bob was referring to the jury. They would be reviewing everything you did and decide on whether you did it according to the law and within the policies and procedures of your organization. For some odd reason, this inspired me. I never felt so alive as I did when upholding the laws and our constitution.

My last week at this internship was by far the most exciting. We were sent to a residence with a search and arrest warrant for a cocaine dealer. "Beaver County Narcotics," Bob hollered, as he banged on the door. "We got a warrant."

No one replied. Bob banged again before he motioned for one of the guys to come to break the door in. Didn't take but one kick to bust the rotted hinges open. "Spread out and search," Bob ordered. The smell of rot and human fouler permeated through the outside of the dwelling.

"Housekeeper must have the day off," Shoo joked.

I took the job of searching the kitchen. The linoleum floor was caked in what looked like dried stew from the 1960s. Garbage was strewn across the counters, and dirty dishes filled the sink. I waved my hand in front of my face. It smelled like moldy cheese and dirty socks. I moved a large empty box from the counter onto the floor. A cockroach scurried from beneath. I jumped 20 feet. *Keep it together, Ray!*

I could not believe people lived like this. It was like nothing I had ever seen before. I gagged as I began my search. I opened the refrigerator. It smelled as if they were storing a dead body, but all I could see was beer. I started on the cabinets. I stuck my hand in each and swept them empty. Nothing of concern. I opened the last cabinet. I reached my hand onto the top shelf and found something. I was excited. I may have just found the dope! I pulled out my find.

"Ahhhhh!!!!!" I screamed like a baby. It was not the dope. It was a dead rat. I dropped the rodent to the ground. My heart was pounding. Shoo came running into the room.

"You scared of a little mouse, Morrow?" Shoo asked, laughing.

"Funny, Shoo real funny. I'm probably going to get some terrible disease," I said, trying to blow it off.

"Stop being a baby. It's just a little dirt," Shoo said, smirking.

"The dirtier, the better!" Bob laughed, appearing in the doorway. Bob loved the art of the search. It was like an intense game of hide-and-seek to him. The bigger the mess, the more spots to look, the bigger the thrill.

"Found the true trash," one of the officers yelled from the back.

He had found the suspect passed out in a back room. The agent dragged his weak, wobbly body out into the living room, drool dripping down his chin. In less than 5 minutes, Bob was able to get the half-unconscious guy to show us where the drugs and money were. The search was over.

I was given the assignment of writing up the report on the hunt. I was excited to have the responsibility of my first report. I was head down, pencil moving when Bob approached.

"I should be done in about an hour," I said.

Bob nodded, "Don't forget to write about the rat," he said, only half-kidding.

Spring 1977

My second internship at the Ellwood Police Department. Ellwood City was a small and close-knit community. I was born in Ellwood City and lived there for the first eight years of my life before moving to Hopewell. We moved to Hopewell in January of 1963. I was in third grade. Both of my parents were from Ellwood, and their families still lived in that same small town. I was excited to come back to my roots. I knew the sleepy little town of Ellwood City well. I figured there was no better place to learn to be a hometown police officer than in your first hometown.

I stayed with my Aunt Helen, my mother's older sister. My Aunt Helen was the spitting image of my mother. She also felt free to yell at me or discipline me any time she thought it was necessary. It was like a home away from home.

My cousin Jeff, who was just a few years younger than I, was also living at home. He was kind enough to share his room with me during my stay. Even though my time was often occupied, it was great fun, staying up late and spending time together.

I worked all three shifts and found the midnight shift to be the most entertaining. Nothing happened during the days in Ellwood. Literally nothing. But luckily, I was put under the tutelage of Lieutenant Thomas Magnifico. Lt. Magnifico loved being a policeman and, more than anything, loved helping people. And while not much happened, Lt. Magnifico taught me that even the most mundane duties of law enforcement required passion and commitment.

It was 7 am on a Saturday. I was on duty. I didn't expect

much to go down that day. I had drunk my second cup of coffee, but still, my eyelids dipped. I fought back the sleep. I may have stayed up a little too late last night. I must have nodded off when a large hand banged on my metal desk. I shot straight up. "Yes, sir," I said, not even sure who was waking me.

"Morrow. You awake?" Magnifico asked.

"Of course," I replied, swallowing my yawn.

"Good! The call came in from the American Standard Credit Union off Second Street. You want to take the call?" Magnifico asked.

"Absolutely," I said, jumping up.

The credit union was adjacent to the small factory that employed a lot of the men in the town. They had called because their safe had been broken in to and the contents emptied. And while it wasn't as exciting as narcotics, this was a very important matter in such a quaint town. So important that the local newspaper, "The Ellwood City Ledger," sent a reporter and photographer to the crime scene. They took my picture, inspecting the safe, and wrote a story that made the front page the very next day. There I was in my light blue leisure suit on the cover of the newspaper. I studied the photo and shook my head; *Inspector Erskine would never have worn a blue leisure suit.*

May 1977

Even though most of my time was spent building my career, I did manage to have a little fun during my senior year in college. On several occasions, my buddies and I took the ride to Ohio, where the drinking age was still 18. There was a nightclub we would go to call the Aquanaut. The Aquanaut was a nightclub that had liquor, live bands, and lots of women. A young-blooded college student could not ask for more.

On this occasion, several of us headed to the Aquanaut. The Aquanaut was only 30 minutes past the Pennsylvania border, and many of my hometown friends ran there for a good time. When we arrived, we found that there were several girls there from Hopewell. I knew most of the girls, but there was one that I had never seen before. My eyes caught her eyes. I turned away; my face flushed. She was the most beautiful girl I had ever seen before. She had long blonde hair, big brown eyes, she reminded me of the Van Morrison song, "Brown Eyed Girl." This girl possessed the most beautiful smile and had quite an attractive figure. My heart was pounding fast. Sweat began to form on my brow.

"Who is that girl?" I asked my friend, Joe.

"That's Lynn Oesterling. You don't know her?" he asked.

I shook my head no, "But I need to know her," I mumbled.

"What? I can't hear you?" my friend hollered over the music.

I walked up to her, a smile across my round face. I pushed back my brown hair. I went in as smoothly as possible. "Can I buy you, girls, a drink?" I asked the group, trying to impress.

Lynn turned down my offer, her three friends immediately accepted. I tried to talk to her again. And again, she shrugged me off. Twelve bucks for those drinks, and it did not get me anywhere with Lynn. That was over half the money I had for the night. I decided that for twelve dollars, I was going to talk to her.

Even though she had turned down my offer to buy her a drink, I was not deterred. After a few minutes of small talk with her friends, I went over to Lynn. I was going to try again.

"Would you like to dance?" I asked, extending my hand like the prince in Cinderella.

"No, thank you," she said flatly.

I graciously smiled and walked away, kind of relieved that I did not have to dance. I was not that smooth or light on my feet as they used to say. Another turndown. Crazy as it sounds, at that moment, I knew that she and I were going to date. I was not going to let this moment pass.

I went back to my friend and started asking questions about this beautiful girl. I found out that she went to nursing school. So, I used that as my in.

I stood up straighter and headed towards the bar where she sat with her friends. "Excuse me," I said. "Lynn, right?" She smiled and nodded as she took a sip of her drink. "I'm Ray."

"I know," she said, her lips beginning to turn upwards into a smile.

"I hear you are going to be a nurse." She smiled again and pulled the bar seat next to her out for me. It worked she finally opened up, and we talked for a while and then Lynn and her friends left.

I drove back to Ellwood City that night. I had to work in the morning. I crawled into my bed at about three o'clock in the morning. Jeff was sleeping in the bed next to mine, but for some reason, I felt compelled to wake him up, "Jeff. Jeff!"

"What, man? It's 3 am," he said groggily.

"I met the girl I am going to marry," I said.

"Whatever," he said, and went right back to sleep. Jeff was not as excited as I was that I had found the girl I was going to marry.

CHAPTER

May 1977

"Your father and I are so proud of you, Ray," my mom said as she adjusted my Oxford cap.

"If the only grandfather could see you now. The first man in our family to graduate from college," my dad said, the pride splashed across his face.

"Thank you," I said as I hugged my mom. It was hard to believe that this day had actually come. I was graduating with a degree in law enforcement and was one step closer to becoming an FBI agent.

"Ready, Morrow?" Shoo called from the back room where we had gathered before the ceremony. We were fortunate enough to be able to graduate from the Penn State Beaver campus. "Next time we see you guys, we will be college graduates," Shoo told my parents.

My mom gave us a wave as we walked out towards the amphitheater. There were over 100 graduates from all different areas of study. As the Dean of the Penn State Beaver

Campus started to call the names of the graduating students, it began to sink in. I kept thinking to myself. I did it. I'm an adult. As my name was called, I walked onto the stage, feeling very proud of myself. The very first to graduate on the Morrow side of the family.

That night, I returned to my Aunt Helen's, packed my bags, and returned home. It was nearly 1 am when I arrived back and my parents' house. When I walked in the front door, my dad was waiting for me in his chair. A smile crosses his aging face. I couldn't have been more proud.

With school done, so was my financial aid, and the most financially responsible decision was to move home and save money. Lynn and I were dating now, and I needed the money. I enjoyed nothing more than taking Lynn out to dinner, a movie whatever it was I just loved to make her laugh and smile. She had a beautiful smile and an infectious laugh.

I started my new job right after graduation, working as a security guard at the Penn State Beaver campus. I was making approximately $9,000 a year. Not a bad living for the time.

Lynn would come to visit me when I worked the 3-11 shift. She often brought me something to eat and would hang around while for a while. Often she would see me herding the ducks from Brodhead Road back to the little lake where they lived. I would look over at her and see her laughing as I painstaking convinced these ducks to get back to the lake. I would think to myself as I had to stop traffic and get this group of ducks off the road and back on to campus if this was how Inspector Erskine got his start.

It didn't take long for duck herding to get old, so Shoo

and I decided to apply to the FBI. We were applying for the position of File Clerk GS-3, about the most entry-level job you can find in the FBI.

My father was furious when he found out I had applied to the FBI in Washington D.C., "You are going to go to Washington D.C.?" he asked, his brow furrowed.

"That is where the FBI is headquartered," I said.

"Ray, you have a good job. Why would you travel to Washington for such low pay? Your mother said you will only be making $5,600 a year. That is so much less than you are making now. And you will have to pay for a place to live," he said, trying to convince me.

I had spent most of my life reminding my father of my dream, so I wasn't surprised that I was going to have to do it again. I went into the same spiel I had been giving him for years when my mother interrupted, "What about Lynn? Won't she be upset if you move?"

I was persistent and had convinced Lynn that dating me would be in her best interest. We had been dating for over six months now and had grown very close. I had not yet told her that I was planning on moving over five-hours away. I wasn't sure how she would take it, and I certainly wasn't looking forward to upsetting her.

"I'm not sure, mom. I am going to talk to her about it when I know I have the job," I said.

I checked the mail every day, waiting for a reply from the FBI. Three weeks later, I opened up the mailbox. There it was. The return address read: FEDERAL BUREAU

OF INVESTIGATION, J. Edgar Hoover Building, 935 Pennsylvania Avenue, Washington D.C. 20535. My heart stopped. The FBI. The letter. I held my breath as I tore it open. There it was in boldface:

WELCOME TO THE FBI. We are pleased to inform you that you have been chosen for the position of File Clerk GS3. You are to report to the J. Edgar Hoover Building on August 22, 1977.

I raced into the house, yelling for my father. I was ecstatic. He instantly knew why I was so excited. He was far from happy, but he knew he couldn't hold me back any longer.

"You should tell Lynn today," was all he said.

I decided the best way to break the news was at Lynn's favorite restaurant, the Wooden Angel in Beaver, PA. I waited until after dinner, and as we waited for dessert, I broke the news.

"You know how much I love you and how great I think everything has been going, right?" I said, trying to soften the blow of leaving.

"Yeah," she said, putting down her fork, the side of her mouth twisting. She knew me so well at this point and figured that was not the end of it.

"And you know that I have always wanted to be an FBI agent, right?"

"Believe you have told me that a time or two," she said with a smirk.

"And you know I want…"

Lynn interrupted me, "What are you trying to say, Ray?"

"I got a job in Washington, D.C. I leave in two weeks," I said, spitting it out.

Her mouth twisted back up; her eyes squinted. This was her unhappy face. I had only seen it a few times in our months of dating, but I knew it. "You're just going to move? Leave me?" she asked, her tone flat.

"I am not leaving you. I am going to work for the FBI," I corrected.

"But you are leaving Hopewell, right?" she asked.

"I am," I said.

"And you are only telling me now because?"

She had a point. I could have told her earlier, but I was scared. Plus, I didn't even know if I would get the job because there were so many applicants, and I figured there was no point in making her mad before I knew for sure. But she was right. I should have told her earlier. She was a rational woman, and I was sensible enough to know she had the right to be upset about that, and I told her so.

"What if I tell you I don't want you to go?" she asked.

"I am following my dream, the dream I had since I was a kid. I want you to part of that dream," I replied.

She took a deep breath. "If this is what you want, Ray, I will support you."

We decided to let the relationship play out long-distance for a year, and then we would go from there. We both knew that it wouldn't be easy, but if this was meant to be, then it was meant to be.

I was finishing up my last week of work at Penn State Beaver, on August 16, 1977, I was working the 3-11 shift, and Lynn stopped by to see me. When she got out of the car, I noticed her ever-present smile was gone. She walked towards me and could barely get out the words, "Elvis died." I was shocked, stunned. How could this be? He was so young. For a short while, I forgot all about those damn ducks. What a sad day.

♥ ♥ ♥

On August 20, 1977, Shoo and I packed our bags and then packed his 1974 Red 2 door Mercury Comet. We set off east down the PA Turnpike, then I 70 to Washington D.C. I was ecstatic. I had made it to the FBI. Not as a Special Agent, but I was sure that once they saw me, they would immediately correct their mistake and make me a Special Agent. They just had to. The radio blared Bob Seger's Rock and Roll Never Forgets as my mind wandered.

"Don't worry about the money, they're going to make us Special Agents right after we get there," Shoo said, while we were somewhere in Maryland. I smiled. He knew it, too.

We pulled into Washington D.C. as we had reservations for the first week to stay at the Hotel Harrington hotel right across the street from the J. Edgar Hoover Building. The hotel was far from grand. It was old in a way that lacked luster. It has been called the oldest operating hotel in Washington, D.C. It was outdated, even by 1977's standards, and most of the rooms were dark and dingy with red carpets and flowery curtains and bedspreads, but the price was just right for Shoo and me, and there was a bar in the hotel. We began driving around the city, aimlessly to see where we were going to live permanently.

"So, where we gonna live?" I asked.

"I dunno," Shoo said. This was his response to almost every question I asked him.

We had not planned this well. We drove around the town, up and down the side streets. Then across the bridge into Alexandria, Virginia.

"There," I said, pointing at a FOR RENT sign in front of a small apartment complex.

Shoo's upper lip went up in disgust. The building was old and close to dilapidation. Most of the paint that covered the wood was peeling. And the shutters that remained were holding on for dear life.

"We can probably afford it," I said with a shrug.

"They should pay us to live there," Shoo retorted.

The building manager was sitting in a tiny office. The man took a drag of his cigarette and greeted us. "Can I help you?"

"We are looking for a place to live," Shoo said.

"I got one apartment. It is a one-bedroom, one bathroom. It's small but clean," he said.

He walked us up to the second floor. It was small and not quite as clean as he said. But it worked.

"We'll take it," I said. Shoo just stared at me and grumbled.

It was far from fancy, but I didn't care. Here we were in the Nation's Capital, working for the premier law enforcement agency in the world.

On August 22, 1977, we reported working at the J. Edgar Hoover Building at 6:30 am. I was in awe of the massive office building. The exterior was a typical office building, but the inside was a maze. This made it all the more alluring at first. Allure quickly grew to annoyance as we had to learn to navigate and decipher hallways and room numbers that didn't align due to the odd shape of the building. The halls were long, and doors lined every few feet. Elevators were hard to find. I had to make a mental map to ensure I would be at my workstation on the eleventh floor on time. To my pleasant surprise, the halls were lined with framed movie posters. Jimmy Stewart's *The FBI Story*, James Cagney's *G-Men*, Alfred Hitchcock's *The Man Who Knew Too Much*, and many more.

After a few months, both Shoo and I decided to work the graveyard shift, 4:30 pm- 1:00 am. This shift came with higher pay, less traffic, and free parking at the Smithsonian.

As file clerks, we were both assigned to the FBI's Identification Division ("IDENT"). This meant that we would be looking at fingerprints all night. We had to sort and file them correctly according to their classification. Neither of us knew what our job would entail, but we can both agree, we were expecting something a little more exciting than what we were thrown into.

After several months of playing the role of glorified file clerks, Shoo and I applied to be fingerprint examiners. Within weeks we were enrolled in the fingerprint examiner class. Only the most experienced fingerprint examiners served as training instructors, and they took this very seriously. Shoo and I, on the other hand, did not. Were just biding time until they made us Special Agents.

We spent our nights with our eye on a magnifying glass examining fingerprints. We literally counted and classified every loop, whirl, swirl, and ridge. All night long, we counted and classified. About 11 months into the job, they had still not made us Special Agents, and the monotony was making me go insane.

It didn't take long for fingerprints to lose their luster, so Shoo and I both started to apply for other jobs with other federal agencies and local police departments in the Washington D.C. area. We utilized our time during the day before we had to go to work to apply to the various agencies. Being in D.C. was excellent. It was like eating from a buffet. There were many career opportunities, unlike back home, where there wasn't much to offer except for the steel mills.

The Alexandria VA Police Department hired Shoo. I was hired by the U.S. Secret Service Uniformed Division assigned to the White House to protect the President and First Family. I figured my dad would have to be proud of me if I was protecting the President of the United States.

January 1978

It was my father's 50th birthday, and I went home to celebrate with my family.

"This is a lovely restaurant, Ray," my mother said.

"Too nice for a clerk salary," my father grunted.

I hadn't yet told them about having applied to the U.S. Secret Service Uniformed Division and that they were in the process of conducting my background investigation. I hadn't planned on doing that tonight. Tonight, I had a different surprise for them.

"How is your food?" I asked Lynn, ignoring my father.

"It's great," she said, dabbing her mouth with a napkin.

"Are you okay, Ray?" my mother asked.

"I'm okay, mom."

"Your face is all red and your sweating," my sister Violet chimed in.

"I'm fine," I reiterated.

I wasn't okay. In fact, I was extremely nervous. I was planning on asking Lynn to marry me when we finished eating. We had been carrying on this long-distance relationship long enough. At least as far as I was concerned. But we hadn't talked about marriage. I wasn't sure if she was even ready. I barely ate. My stomach was in knots.

"Would you mind taking Violet home with you? Your mother and I are going to stop at Vince and Mary Pat Horne's house after we leave the restaurant," my father said.

"Absolutely!" Lynn said.

"NO! No, we can't!" I sputtered.

Everyone looked at me as if I had lost my mind.

"Why can't you take your sister home, aren't you going there anyway?" my mother asked.

I came up with the only thing I could think of, "Lynn and I are supposed to go to a surprise party for Ed Wilamowski. It was a secret, and I was not supposed to tell Lynn because she was good friends with one of Ed's sisters."

"Why is he having a surprise party?" my mom asked, confused.

I began to stammer, "I don't know. I was just told to be there."

"Really?" Lynn asked, confused. "I think we can still take her home."

Again, I explained this idiotic excuse about being there on time and not being late, and still, I got a dumbfounded look from Lynn.

34

"We will take Violet," my mother said, more frustrated than confused.

We walked out to the parking lot. "You were ridiculous in there," Lynn said to me. I started to stutter. I could tell Lynn was upset with me. My initial plan was to drive Lynn to Moraine State Park, where we had gone on our first date. But I could tell Lynn would be angry with me if I waited any longer. So right there in the parking lot of the restaurant Rusty Nail in New Brighton, Pennsylvania I pulled out the card I had written my poem on and read it to her:

"When we first met, I knew you were the one.
I knew my search for the love of my life was done.
Your beautiful big brown eyes and long blonde hair.
I just felt someone like you was very rare.

Our first meeting did not go so well
But somehow, I knew there would be a wedding bell.
Your grace and charm and angelic beauty
To me, you were more than just another cutie.

Together we have made this long-distance relationship work
And at this time our relationship has come to a fork
So now I ask you with the utmost happiness and glee

Will you marry me?" I finished, dropping to one knee.

A smile like I had never seen crossed her angelic face. Tears welled up in her brown eyes. "Yes, Ray Morrow, I will marry you!"

I could not believe it. The girl of my dreams just agreed

to spend the rest of her life with me. I rose from my knee, displayed the ring, and kissed her.

"Now, you should tell your parents why you were such a jerk in there," she said with a smile.

The Horne's didn't live far from the restaurant. I pulled into their driveway behind my parent's car. We walked to the door, hand in and hand. When we arrived, my parents were dumbfounded and confused as to why Lynn and I were there.

"Why are you here, son?" my father asked, still annoyed from dinner.

"We're getting married!" I exclaimed. The look on my parent's faces was exceptional, I knew right away they were excited for me and happy that I was able to convince someone as lovely as Lynn to say yes to my marriage proposal.

CHAPTER

A few months after our engagement, I had even more big news to share.

"Guess what?" I said to Lynn over the phone.

"You're coming home?" she asked, hopeful.

"I'm not," I replied. Her response sort of killed my news. We were still living apart; Lynn in Pittsburgh and I was in Virginia. It was hard, and I knew she was struggling. She was working full time as a nurse at a local hospital, but I could tell she was lonely. I had only seen her a few times since our engagement. So, I understood her reaction. "No. I'm sorry. But I still have good news."

"What is it?" she said. I could tell she was forcing herself to smile.

"I was accepted to the Secret Service," I said.

"That is great, hon. I'm happy for you."

"This is good for us! I should soon be making enough for us to get a place," I told her, trying to be uplifting.

"That would be nice," she said sincerely. "Think you will get to meet the President?" she asked.

"I hope so!"

August 1978

I started my first eight weeks of training the following week. The training was in Beltsville, Maryland, at the U.S. Secret Service Training Facility. The focus of the first part of the training was firearm protocol, safety, and accuracy. I had never shot a gun, but I was aware of some of the basics.

The Secret Service used the standard target shooting with a handgun, an Uzi submachine gun, and a shotgun from various distances. They also taught combat and close-quarters shooting as well. I was able to witness and learn from some of the best sharpshooters in the world. By the time the class wrapped, I not only knew how to shot a gun but also clean a firearm, break it down and put it back together. I had achieved an accuracy of over 90%. Not quite a skilled marksman, but not bad.

There was also a three-day intense crammer course at the University of Maryland Fire School. This training focused on the duties and responsibilities of being a fireman. Based on what I learned at the University of Maryland Fire School, I have the utmost respect and admiration for what Firemen do for a living. We were exposed to being in a smoke-filled room with very little oxygen and virtually no visibility and being tasked with finding someone who needed to be extracted from the room and then getting them safely out of the room. It was frightening. We also learned firsthand what it was like to carry all their necessary equipment up several flights of stairs and then how to properly store the equipment. I have to say what they do daily is nothing short of heroic. It was some of the most intense training I had ever been through and several moments that scared the living hell out of me. True heroes.

The next six weeks of training were at the Federal Law Enforcement Training Center ("FLETC") in Glynco, Georgia, which serves as the Headquarters Facility for FLETC. There are well over 1,500 acres of land and numerous buildings and firearms ranges, dining hall, workout facilities, driver training courses all in all an awe-inspiring place to learn.

FLETC's main objective is to train the vast majority of federal agents and officers who work in a variety of areas of law enforcement to include; security, terrorism, border security, immigration enforcement, etc. This training was similar to a military boot camp.

The last two weeks of our training were back at the Beltsville, MD training facility. This is where the preparation for our assignments became more detailed. The White House had its procedures and protocols as did the Embassies, and we needed to have a good understanding of those before we reported for our first day on the job.

The two months of training flew by, and on November 9, 1978, The U.S. Secret Service Uniformed Division held a graduation ceremony for our class. My mother, father, and Lynn came to Maryland to attend the ceremony. The ceremony was just like my college graduation. We all sat in our spiffy uniforms and listened to numerous speeches about what we would encounter as we entered into this next phase of our career. They called us up one by one and presented us with our badges and certificates.

After graduation, my father came to me and asked, "Can I have a picture with you in your uniform?"

"Of course, dad," I replied.

My mother took a picture of us. The smile on my father's face was something to behold. I can't ever remember him smiling that way ever before. "I'm so proud of you, son," he said and hugged me.

Not being a Pharmacist turned out to be okay after all.

CHAPTER

5

November 1978

I was assigned to the White House to protect President, Jimmy Carter, and his family. I got chills just thinking about that. And my father, a proud democrat, was ecstatic. This was the first time I could remember my father genuinely being proud of my career choice.

Shoo and I left our shitty little apartment in Alexandria, VA, and we're now living with five other guys in a large house in Fairfax, Virginia. Shoo, and I had recruited friends to live with us to split rent and bills. The house was a large, split level with five bedrooms, three bathrooms, and a finished basement that included a fireplace. It was in a charming well-established neighborhood. Shoo and I met our roommates Walter Sanders, Paul Champion, Donny Bates, Ken Nedved, and Bren McStay, who we called Smooth while working at the FBI. Four of our roommates still worked for the FBI. Shoo was now a Police Officer with the Alexandria, Virginia Police Department.

The first day at the White House was surreal. I reported to the Secret Service Uniformed Division's breakroom at 7 am sharp. The breakroom was located in the basement of the East Wing of the Whitehouse. This is where we would report each morning and wait for our daily assignments.

Each morning began with the Lieutenant providing a briefing, announcing our initial assignment, identifying the security post where each of us would start our shift. From there, we would start our protection rotation schedule for the day. There were security posts throughout the White House and grounds, and we would move every hour to a new post, and each post had its designation. Each security post was slightly different in its areas of responsibility. Still, vigilance, awareness, and dedication to your duties and responsibilities were keys to keeping the President and the First family safe.

"Morrow," Lieutenant Shubert barked.

"Yes, sir," I replied, stepping forward, straightening my uniform shirt and tie.

"Today, you will start at the Southwest Gate," he ordered.

When positioned at the Southwest Gate, we monitored the vehicle gate entrance and the area surrounding the gate. My job was to keep pedestrian traffic moving and to keep people from gathering and standing in that area. I was also responsible for checking vehicles attempting to enter. Vehicle checks included positively identifying the driver and occupants of the vehicle, searching under the car with mirrors for contraband. This gate was also responsible for securing the area whenever the President or dignitary left the White House Grounds through this gate. And whenever President Carter went jogging on the south grounds, we had to go outside the gate to ensure no pedestrians stopped or stood near the gate or fence area.

"Yes, sir," I replied, stepping back into line.

During a full shift, the officers would move every hour from one post to another. Some of the posts were inside, and others were outside. As I moved along from one post to another, I would get to see the President, the First Lady, Chip Carter, Amy Carter, National Security Advisor, Zbigniew Brzezinski, and Chief of Staff Hamilton Jordan buzzing about.

Working at the White House assigned to protect the President, First Family, and the White House and grounds was a distinct privilege, and to this day, I hold that opportunity in great reverence. It takes a great deal to protect the President of the United States, the First Family and the White House grounds is an incredible undertaking. The people that perform these duties are the best of the best. I will forever be grateful to those who perform and carry out these essential duties and responsibilities each day.

While working at the White House, I had the privilege of working with another individual who has remained a dear friend and confidant and strong advocate for law enforcement, Jack Cahill. Jack was already assigned to the U.S. Secret Service Uniformed Division's White House Detail when I arrived. Jack had a zest for life and learning. He was such a pleasure to work with and to spend my free time with. Jack and I quickly became close friends. Jack and his wife Pam have remained close friends to Lynn and me, and I still go to Jack when I need advice on certain matters.

March 26, 1979

I had arrived at the White House earlier than usual. I knew that today would make the history books, and I was going to play a small part in making the event go smoothly.

"Morrow," Lieutenant barked, "you are to report to North East lawn area and work the crowd and the press located in that area."

The Briefing that morning was more intense than most. There was to be heavy security for this event, and everyone had to be extremely focused. Each assignment was gone over in great detail. The significance of this event was stressed over and over again. As with every protective detail, the Secret Service is involved in there were no stones left unturned. Photos of individuals who may cause a problem were distributed and posted. Everyone entering the White House grounds that day received intense scrutiny. The Secret Service is the absolute best when it comes to protecting their assigned dignitaries. Watching all of this come together after months of preparation and planning was something to behold.

The North East lawn was directly in sight of the stage where the signing of the Peace Treaty was to take place. I was ecstatic. My position would allow me to witness the signing of the Middle East Peace Treaty with President Carter, the President of Egypt, Anwar Sadat, and the Israeli Prime Minister, Menachem Begin. Most of our senators, members of Congress, and other dignitaries were on hand, as was the press. The President gave a brief speech that was followed by both Sadat and Begin speaking.

The Peace Treaty was signed sixteen months after Anwar

44

Sadat's visit to Israel and among other things featured mutual recognition, cessation of the state of war that had existed for quite some time and the normalization of relations between the two countries and the complete withdrawal of Israeli's Armed forces from the Sinai Peninsula.

During the actual signing of the Peace Treaty, all three leaders offered prayers that the treaty would bring peace to the Middle East. The ceremony itself went off without a hitch, and you could feel a sense of relief in the crowd even though it did not ultimately end the differences between the two leaders. This was a day that went down in the history books, and there I was, a young kid from Hopewell witnessing this historic event firsthand.

April 27, 1979

I couldn't believe that I had finally made it. I knew that tomorrow was going to change my life in the best way possible. I had worked the 3-11 shift at the White House and was tired, but my excitement overtook my exhaustion. I decided to leave straight from work. I figured I would be back in Hopewell around 3 am. I drove south on I-95, then headed for the I-495 Beltway, which would get me out of Washington on my way back to Hopewell. I should be home in time to get enough sleep.

The roads were clear, and I began to speed, I figured the more rest I could get the better. I was flying, making great time when I heard sirens blaring behind me. "Should be fine," I mumbled to myself. The Virginia State Trooper approached my window. I figured I would just show him my

Secret Service badge and credentials and explain I am driving home after finishing my shift at the White House and that I was heading home to get married. He would have to understand and provide me with a 'professional courtesy.' After about 20 minutes, I was headed back to Hopewell with my speeding ticket in hand.

Four hours later, I arrived at my parents' home. I used the key I still had and quietly snuck in and tucked myself into the guest bed. I had six hours to rest up before my wedding.

♥ ♥ ♥

April 28, 1979

"You nervous?" my father asked, peeking his head into the room.

"Not even a little," I replied, a smile sprawling across my face.

"Good. I wasn't nervous when I married your mom, either."

"All I can hope is that our marriage is half as blessed as yours," I said, smiling at him.

My dad responded by saying one of his favorites, "Ray, a happy marriage is the direct result of hard work, sacrifice, and understanding. I know you two will have a happy and blessed life."

My best man and cousin, Anthony Pietrcollo, popped his head into the room, "It's time."

My father placed his hand on my shoulder. "I am so proud of you, son."

I felt a sense of pride sweep over me. Here I was in law

enforcement and not counting pills, and he was still proud of me. I wrapped my arms around him, hugging him. He patted me on the back.

"Your bride is waiting."

The music started, and Lynn began the wedding march to the altar at Our Lady of Fatima Church in Hopewell. I stood in front of Father Coyne, my family, and God waiting for Lynn to approach. The music changed, and my beautiful bride appeared at the end of the hall. Her sheer veil hung over her angelic face. My heart stopped. I felt a surge of love flow through my body in a way I had never felt before. Her father, Bob, walked her down the aisle and brought her to me.

"Who gives this woman away?" Father Coyne asked.

"I do," her father, Bob replied. He lifted her veil. I could see the joy in her big, beautiful brown eyes.

"You look beautiful," I whispered. She smiled.

We said our 'I do's' in front of 300 people in our hometown. The party that followed consisted of lots of dancing, eating, drinking, cookie tables filled with homemade cookies, and pasta dishes made by several of our guests. The night was perfect.

This moment not only brought us together as man and wife, but it was the first time we were going to live in the same city, we were now connected forever. We bought a small townhouse in Dale City, Virginia. The day after the wedding, Lynn and I headed off on our honeymoon- a four-day cruise. While on our cruise, we stopped at Paradise Island. Lynn and I stayed on the beach and in the water the entire day. That night we attended a luau, and as we were waiting in the buffet line, I passed out cold. They rushed me back to the boat. The ship's doctor came to our room. I had a case of sun poisoning. They packed me in ice, trying to get my body temperature down and made me stay that way, packed in ice, through the entire next day. Here I am on my honeymoon packed in ice while my new wife was out with another couple who had been our table partners at dinner.

Lynn had a blast as they went sightseeing that day. The only sight I saw was the ceiling in our cabin. Our cruise was followed by three days in Disney World. I had never been and was excited to see the amusement park. We took our turn on the "It's a Small World" ride. We were slowly making our way down the water path when the boats broke down.

"You have to be kidding me," I muttered.

Lynn laughed, "I am sure they will get us moving in a few moments," she said, always the optimist.

She was wrong. We were stuck for what seemed like an eternity. As the song played over and over again, and the little figures continued to dance and wave. I never wanted to hear that song again.

Then it was back to our new home to start our lives together.

October 6, 1979

Lynn and I had been living together as man and wife for almost six months. Things were going well. Every day was a honeymoon. That is every day we got to see each other. I worked long hours at the White House, and she worked at Fairfax Hospital in Fairfax, VA.

"Have a good day at work," Lynn said, her eyes closed.

"You too," I said as I kissed her on the cheek and pulled the blankets over her shoulders. She had come off a late shift, and I was starting early. That was our typical routine. But at least we were together. I gave her a final look as I walked out the door and got my head on straight. It was going to be a crazy day at the White House.

Today was the first time a Pope had ever visited the White House. We had prepared for this event for weeks. Extraordinary precautions were taken, and security throughout the Washington D.C. area was extremely tight. Just getting to work that morning, we had to go through several checkpoints. This was going to be a huge event.

I arrived early to my shift and waited in the break room for the Lieutenant to tell me my first assignment of the day. I was so excited. As a devout catholic, there was no greater honor than to be in the presence of the Pope. Lieutenant Shubert did roll call, and I was assigned to the North Grounds of the White House working the Press Corps area. Security Checks at the gates were very tight, and as people entered in, they started to assemble in the guest and press areas. There were people everywhere, and the excitement was in the air. It was palpable. As I worked to keep the press in their area, which is akin to herding cats, I met two priests who were from the United States but were invited to travel with the Pope's contingent while the Pope was in Washington D.C. These two priests started to engage me in conversation, asking questions about the White House, the President, my job, and they talked about their time with the Pope. I continued to keep the press where they belonged to while I carried on my conversation with the two priests.

"I am a practicing Catholic," I told the Priests.

"Do you have a medal of Jesus?" the older Priest asked.

"I do." I pulled the medallion out from under my shirt and showed them. "My parents gave this to me at my Confirmation."

The older Priest took the medallion and held it in his hand. "Would you like me to have your medal blessed by the Pope?"

Tears welled in my eyes. "Yes. Yes, please," I stammered.

He held his hand out as I undid the clasp at my neck. I took the necklace off and let it fall into his hand. The Priest clasped his hand tightly around my medal. "I promise we will get this back to you tomorrow." I trusted them implicitly, with my medal, I mean they were priests. How could I not trust them? As the Pope and President exited the North Portico of the White House, I was able to make eye contact with Pope John Paul. Actual eye contact. My heart swelled to be in his presence. I couldn't wait to call my mom and tell her. Everyone in Hopewell is going to be hearing about this.

When the Pope and President Carter made their way out to the stage, the President welcomed the Pope in Polish. I was awestruck. Then Pope John Paul responded in English. It was amazing. At one point, as President Carter was praising the Pontiff, Pope John Paul clasped his hands together and touched his heart. This brought me to tears, which I quickly wiped away. *You can't be protecting the Pope and the President with tears in your eyes.*

I never thought I would ever have an opportunity to witness an event as historical as this. Nor did I ever believe I would be honored with the duty of protecting the President of The United States and the Pope at the same time.

The next day these same two priests came back to the White House, specifically looking for me. I was called up to the Northwest Gate of the White House, where they handed me my medal with a card from Pope John Paul. In the note, Pope John Paul thanked me for helping to make his visit a safe one, and he wished me well and asked me to stay strong in my Catholic faith.

"Thank you. Thank you both so much," I said, tears trickling down my face. "I can't tell you how honored and humbled I am."

I put the medallion back around my neck and vowed never to take it off again.

As I slowly began to learn more and more about the job, I took great interest in a group of some of our best officers who were selected and trained to provide tours of the White House. This group was well versed in the history of the White House and regaled the tourists visiting the White House with great symbolic and historical moments that happened in each room the tourists passed through. I decided this was something I wanted to do.

In September of 1979, I was selected to be a member of this group. It required long hours of reading and studying as well as working with some of the real tour guides and walking along with them watching and learning how they entertained the White House visitors daily. I thoroughly relished the opportunity to provide these tourists with an understanding of the significance and historical value of this magnificent house. This was indeed an honor for me, and I embraced this opportunity with the ultimate respect and dignity.

November 1979

As I was wrapping up an afternoon tour of the White House, an officer approached me and instructed me to report to our shift sergeant's office immediately. I walked as quickly as I could to the office, located in the basement of the East Wing. We weren't typically pulled away from the floor unless there was an issue that couldn't wait. When I got there, I was told I had a telephone call from my wife. My heart started pounding. Lynn knew only to call me if it was an emergency. She had never called. No one had ever called me at work.

"Hello?" I said, unsure of why my wife was calling.

"Ray?"

"Lynn? Is everything okay?" I asked, knowing perfectly well it wasn't.

"It's your dad," she paused.

"What is it?"

"He passed away."

I could tell it took everything in her to get those words out. My father was only 51-years- old.

I had no words. My best friend, the man I admired the most was gone. I felt as if someone had yanked my heart right out of my chest. "I will be right home," was the only thing I could manage. Lynn said she had already started to pack. I simply hung up, unable to comprehend what was happening. I rode to work with Jack Cahill that day, and Jack was already in the locker room by the time I had finished changing. Jack had requested to take off the rest of the day so he could take me home.

Lynn and I headed back to Pennsylvania the next day. The funeral was held in Ellwood City at the Samuel Teolis Funeral Home. My mom was in shambles, as was my sister. I knew right then that I had to come home.

CHAPTER

6

After the death of my father, I decided it was time to move back to Pennsylvania. My mom needed help, and Lynn was more than ready to go back home.

But before I could do that, I needed to go back to DC, find a job in Pittsburgh, and give my notice. I was determined to get back home as soon as possible, so I called my old boss at the Penn State Beaver campus, who was retired from law enforcement and had numerous connections. I also spoke with Bob Karwoski and made him aware of my intentions. Bob was now with the Conrail/Norfolk Southern Railway Police Department. It was through these two individuals that I was able to make contact with the heads of security for some of Pittsburgh's large Corporate Headquarters. Companies such as U.S. Steel, ALCOA, Heinz, and Allegheny International were looking for individuals who could provide security for their top-level executives.

I interviewed with both Alcoa and Allegheny International. I preferred Allegheny International and hoped that I would be one of the two Executive Protection Specialist they were going to hire.

My first interview with Allegheny International (AI) was with Mr. John Pintirsch, the Chief of Security. My second interview was with Graemer K. Hilton, President of AI. Mr. Hilton was impressive and one of the most congenial and pleasant individuals I had ever met. Mr. Hilton was a very engaging man, very bright, extraordinarily confident but yet a very humble man. I was thoroughly impressed with Mr. Hilton and not yet having met the other executives. I hoped that I would get the honor of protecting Mr. Hilton.

My third interview was with Mr. Clayton Sweeney, Chief Administrative Officer, and Chief Legal Counsel. Mr. Sweeney was a brilliant legal mind. And while I was impressed with his intelligence, I was not as fond of his dry personality.

My last interview was with Mr. Robert Buckley, Chairman, and CEO of AI. Mr. Buckley was a well-respected corporate leader and businessman. He was a large man with a booming voice, a great mind, and a fantastic sense of humor. Mr. Buckley was the only one at the time who had an Executive Protection Specialist assigned to him already, and it was he who insisted that Messrs. Hilton and Sweeney do the same. I still hoped that if I did get the privilege of working at AI, that I would get to protect Mr. Hilton.

July 1980

"Coming, coming," Lynn yelled at the ringing phone.

She dried her hands on the dishtowel as she grabbed the phone. "Hello. Morrow residence," she said.

"Is this Mrs. Morrow?" the voice asked.

"It is. How can I help you?"

"We are looking for Ray Morrow. I am calling from Alleghany International."

"He isn't home. But I can take a message," she replied.

"Can you please let him know that we are offering him the security job he applied for?"

"He will take it!" she said excitedly.

"Excuse me?"

"He will take the job! I will have him call you as soon as he gets home. Thank you!"

All Lynn had wanted was to go home. She didn't even ask what my starting salary would be or whether they were offering health benefits. Nothing. Lynn didn't care what they were offering. All she knew was that I was accepting. I called them back later that day and had no choice but to accept. Lynn left me no room to bargain or negotiate. I accepted their offer and was told that I would start my new assignment on August 18, 1980.

The next day I went to my supervisor and informed him that I would be submitting my two weeks' notice. He sent me over to 1800 G Street NW Washington, the U.S. Secret Service Headquarters to fill out all of the appropriate paperwork. With that, Lynn and I were off to Pittsburgh.

August 1980

We packed our bags and moved to Cranberry Township in Butler County, 30 minutes from my mother's home. We moved into a new two-story, three-bedroom two and a half

bath home on a cul-de-sac in a new Ryan Home development called Creekwood Commons.

I reported working on August 18th. When I arrived, I was
assigned to Mr. Hilton. Tony Adams, the other newly hired
security expert, would be assigned to Mr. Sweeney. I was
delighted with the assignment.

As an Executive Protection Specialist, it was my job to
protect Mr. Hilton at all times. My days were long, and I
never knew when I left my house in the morning if I would
make it home that night due to an unplanned trip that
would come up in the middle of the day. Often, I would get
the word from Mr. Hilton's secretary, Ms. Patricia Graziano,
that we would be leaving shortly and was not sure when we
would be returning. These unplanned trips sometimes took
us to places like New York City, Los Angles, Chicago, or Hot
Coffee, Mississippi. I learned very quickly that I needed to
keep a packed travel bag in the car at all times, as this happened quite frequently.

Allegheny International ("AI") was a multi-national
conglomerate that owned companies such as Sunbeam,
Wilkinson Sword, True Temper, Scripto, Liquid Air, and
several others and consequently, I traveled quite a bit. Of
course, AI had its own fleet of planes and pilots, so traveling
was never a problem. I enjoyed it and became somewhat
accustomed to it. We made several overseas trips a year to
places like London, Paris, Stuttgart, Frankfurt, Tokyo, Hong
Kong, Sydney, and Melbourne. Places I never imagined I
would ever get to see.

March 1981

I came home from work at my usual time, 7:30 pm. Lynn was waiting for me at the door. Lynn never met me at the door unless I had done something wrong. *Oh boy, what did I do?*

I was just ready to ask her what I did when a smile formed across her flawless face. I was confused. She never smiled when she was mad at me. Her face twisted up in such a way that her lips disappeared.

"Hello," I said, kissing her on the cheek. I kept waiting for her to drop the bomb. But she said nothing as she followed me up to our bedroom. Her silent smile was beginning to make me nervous. I proceeded to get changed as she said nothing.

"Look on the dresser," she said, her smile still wide.

Here it comes, I thought as I reached for a small white thing on the dresser top. I picked up the white piece of plastic and looked at it. All I saw was a plus sign. She began clapping her hands together, but I had no idea why this little thing was making her so giddy.

I looked at her with a confused look on my face. She politely took the little piece of plastic from my hand. "The plus sign means I am pregnant," she said, her eyes glistening.

My confusion quickly turned to delight as we had been hoping and praying for this moment for some time. I hugged her, and we both had tears in our eyes. Privately, I was hoping for a boy, and openly Lynn was hoping for a girl. But we both agreed the most important thing was for the baby to be healthy.

November 25, 1981

It was Thanksgiving eve. Lynn and I were preparing to have Thanksgiving dinner with her family. Lynn had spent the day making mashed potatoes, a green bean casserole, and apple pie. I had arrived home around 7 pm, my typical time. The house smelled delicious from her day of cooking.

"Lynn," I called out as I walked into the house.

"In here," she said, yelling from the living room.

"It smells wonderful."

"Thank you," she said, a smile forming across her face. She was sprawled out across our couch. Her round belly was nearly blocking her view from the television. "I'm tired," she said, rubbing her tummy, "this kid has been kicking up a storm."

I sat down next to her and kissed her stomach. "I can't wait to meet you, little one."

"But hopefully not until after Thanksgiving dinner," she said, giving her tummy another rub.

We went to bed early, as we typically did. At midnight Lynn woke me.

"Ray! Ray!"

"Yes?" I replied, still half asleep.

"It's time," she said.

"It's time!"

Lynn moaned in pain as a contraction came on.

"What can I do to help?" I asked frantically. I was typically well prepared for everything, but right now, I was completely unsure of what to do.

"Get the overnight bag and get dressed," she replied.

I did as I was told, and at 1:30 am, Thursday, November

26, 1981, Thanksgiving morning, we arrived at Sewickley Hospital. My heart was racing. I had never been so nervous in my life. As the nurse wheeled Lynn towards the delivery room, she grabbed my hand and squeezed it. "We got this!" she said, forcing a smile between her contractions. I knew what she meant by that. She was letting me know that she had this, and I was going to do everything in my power to coach without interference.

The hospital informed us that Lynn's obstetrician, Dr. Nix, would arrive in a few hours and that Lynn was not very far along. Lynn proceeded to do what she needed to do, and I did my part by not bothering her. Every now and then, I would show her how to breathe, and she would just give me a dirty look. Eventually, I took the hint; I stopped advising and just held her hand.

Dr. Nix came in around 8:00 am. He told us that Lynn probably had a few more hours until she would push. At that time, I called both our parents and informed them we would not be able to make Thanksgiving dinner but would be bringing home a Thanksgiving baby. Everyone was extremely excited as this would be their first-ever grandchild. I told Lynn's parents to just go on with their plans for Thanksgiving dinner, but they would now need to supplement their dinner with the side dishes and the pies that Lynn was supposed to bring. Our son Ross was born at 1:30 pm Thanksgiving Day. Lynn and I celebrated in the hospital with our baby, and hospital turkey and mashed potatoes. It was perfect.

April 1983

Alleghany International was going to hold its first-ever Annual Share Holders Meeting outside of Pittsburgh. They had decided on New York City, the countries epicenter for big business. I, along with Bob Price, a fellow Executive Protection Specialist, assigned to protect the Chairman and CEO Robert Buckley, worked with members of the New York City Police Department to provide extra security for the event. We were prepared for the protesters that were going to bombard the event and try to disrupt the meeting. As I stated earlier, one of the companies owned by AI was Wilkinson Sword, and one of their subsidiaries produced rubber bullets that were used by the British Army as a form of riot control in Northern Ireland during the unrest.

There were even some threats made against our CEO and President. The day before the event, Bob and I went to the location of the event. We performed our advanced security routine to look over everything and make any final adjustments we felt were necessary.

"This won't work at all," I told Bob, motioning to the seats and dais.

Bob looked around. "You're right."

The way that the event had been set up kept the audience between us and the exit. Plus, the safe room we had requested was nearly 1,000 feet from where the meeting was to take place. If something were to happen, our protectees were as good as dead. We had the entire room layout changed, and we quickly had to identify and secure a new safe room if we needed to get our protectees out in a hurry.

We also made sure that the police would have someone outside both the meeting room and the safe room.

We were able to make all the necessary arrangements to ensure a safe meeting place for our employers. I woke up early the next morning to meet with Bob and discuss the plan once more. We met in the lobby of the Regency Hotel on Park Avenue. Everything about the place was 5 star. I had never experienced such a fancy hotel before. I felt that the occasion and event required a new suit. I had picked one up a week earlier. It was a tannish gray plaid and fit like a glove. I had never had a suit like this before. I caught a glimpse of myself in the glass doors as I walked to meet Mr. Hilton. This was what I had always pictured, me, a real-life Inspector Lewis Erskine

We headed east down 57th Street, towards the New York Athletic Club towards Central Park South approximately ten blocks away from the hotel. I lead Mr. Hilton, Mr. Buckley, and Bob Price followed directly behind them. I stood tall as we made our way down the street. I have to say; I was feeling pretty good at that moment. Then shit happened, literally. A bird pooped on my shoulder. I instantly deflated; here I was about to walk into one of the most important meetings of my life, and I had bird shit on my shoulder. Mr. Buckley having seen this walked up behind me and whispered in my ear,

"They sing for rich people,"

"I don't feel rich right now," I replied.

"Here you go," Mr. Hilton said kindly, as he gave me his handkerchief so I could wipe it off.

I wiped away the white glob, but a small stain remained. But as we approached the building, I had to focus on more important things. There was already a crowd of protesters gathering outside the building. Bob and I escorted Mr. Buckley and Mr. Hilton to a side entrance into the building and then to the meeting room to show them how we set up the room. We then took them to the safe room where they could wait until the meeting was about to start.

When the time came, Bob and I escorted them to the dais, Bob took his position near the dais, and I went towards the back of the room. As the meeting progressed, they started to take questions from the audience. We quickly realized that some of the protesters had made it into the meeting. They were spread throughout the room. The room was divided into two sections. There were fifteen rows of chairs in each section.

The protesters' questions began to get more bellicose, and very quickly, things got out of hand. One of the protesters charged the stage. I yelled to Bob to get our guys out as I body slammed the oncoming rioter. Bob quickly removed Mr. Buckley and Mr. Hilton and immediately escorted them into the safe room. A police officer quickly apprehended the gentlemen I had tackled. He was apprehended and escorted out of the room. Just as the others were fleeing, other police officers arrived on the scene and safely escorted the remaining attendees out of the room.

When I arrived at the safe room, both Mr. Hilton and Mr. Buckley were shaken by the whole incident, and they just wanted to get to the airport and get back to Pittsburgh. With all that was happening, we forgot that their wives still needed to be picked up at the hotel and taken to the airport. Bob and I made arrangements for the wives to be picked up, but we kept Mr. Hilton and Mr. Buckley inside the safe room until the police informed us that the group of protesters that had gathered outside had disbursed. We then escorted our protectees to the car and on to the airport.

When we arrived at the airport, we were informed their wives were already on board. Mr. Buckley and Mr. Hilton got on the plane while Bob and I retrieved our bags from the trunk of the limousine and put them on board in the luggage compartment. We secured the luggage door and made our way onto the airplane. When Bob and I stepped inside, we got a standing ovation from everyone, including the pilots. Both Mrs. Buckley and Mrs. Hilton gave Bob and me a big hug and a kiss on the cheek. It had been quite a day.

April 7, 1985

"Look. Look over there, Ross. Do you see it?" I asked, pointing at the bright pink plastic Easter egg tucked under the evergreen shrub.

Ross toddled over to the bush and picked up the egg and held it high in the air, and let out a loud squeal.

"Good job!" I said, clapping my hands.

"Ray? Ray!" Lynn hollered, waving me over to the back porch.

"Let's go get, Mommy," I said to Ross. I scooped him up and carried him to Lynn. She was pregnant with our second child and was due any minute now.

"You doing okay?" I asked her as I approached.

"I think this little girl may be coming," she said.

"You sure?" I asked.

Two days later, on April 09, 1985, our second son Blake

was born. I can't say Lynn wasn't a little disappointed that we had another boy, but still elated for our new healthy baby.

February 1986

"Have a seat, Ray," Mr. Hilton said, pointing towards the large leather chair situated in front of his Mahogany desk.

I did as I was told. Mr. Hilton and I had enjoyed many conversations in his office, so I wasn't surprised that he had asked me to come to join him for a cup of coffee and a chat.

"How are the kids?" he asked.

"They are great," I said. I wasn't sure why he had asked me that. He and I spoke almost daily, and the kids came up often. I felt like he was procrastinating.

"And Lynn?"

"She is well, too. Thank you for asking." Mr. Hilton didn't reply. "Is everything okay?"

"Yes, Ray. Things are well. Other than I am getting old," he said with a chuckle.

I smiled at him. He was nearly 68 but was in excellent shape for his age. Silver streaked his dark hair; he was physically fit and well put together. He could have easily passed for his early 50's.

"Well, you don't look it, sir," I replied.

"But I am starting to feel it, which is why I have decided to retire. I wanted you to be one of the first to know."

"I appreciate that, Mr. Hilton. I really do. And I appreciate everything you have done for my family and me."

"It was my pleasure, son," he said.

Abdul Kalam had said, *"Let me define a leader. He must have vision and passion and not be afraid of any problem. Instead, he should know how to defeat it. Most importantly, he must work with integrity."*

Mr. Hilton was a true leader, a man of integrity, a man of passion and vision. He never wavered or shied away from any problems or situations. He attacked them with gusto and zeal that was admirable, and he did it all with dignity and respect. Mr. Hilton was one of the greatest men I had ever had the opportunity to work with, to know, and call my friend. And I will be forever grateful.

"When are you retiring?" I asked. Hoping there was time for me to find new employment.

"In August," he replied.

I knew that this had to be my chance to pursue my passion, follow my dream, and finally become an FBI Special Agent.

I decided this was the right time to apply for the FBI. The hiring process to become an FBI Special Agent is an arduous trek. It can take a year or more to get through their comprehensive background investigation. I began by filling out the nine-page application that covered everything and anything you had done since high school. Every neighborhood, every school, every activity was included, as were your parents and siblings, relatives, friends, teachers, coaches, employers. And from that initial information with each interview, the FBI conducted they gathered more information and more people to interview. After I submitted my application, I received a call to meet with the Applicant Recruiter. This interview lasted approximately one hour and was used to gauge my interest and knowledge of the FBI. That interview went very well, and I was more excited than ever, but I knew this was going to be like running a marathon, not a sprint. I prepared myself for the next interview, which was held at the FBI Field Office in Pittsburgh, Pennsylvania, at the Federal Building.

This interview was in front of a three-person panel that included the Applicant Recruiter and two field agents who were trained in the applicant and interviewing process. I also had to squeeze the trigger of a revolver in a timed sequence to ensure I had the hand strength to shoot a firearm. There was also a physical exam I had to take at a nearby high school in which I had to complete a mile and a half run, pushups, sit-ups, and a stair-step test. All had to be scored within the required time or the required amount. Fortunately, I had been training for these and passed with no problem. I thought that if I made it through the process, I might be able to get into an FBI New Agent class at Quantico in late summer. But summer came and went.

In September, I received a call from Bob Karwoski, there was a local law enforcement meeting held at the Aliquippa Country Club, and the Special Agent in Charge of the Pittsburgh FBI Field Office was going to be in attendance. Bob had made arrangements with the Special Agent assigned to the Beaver Resident Agency to have me seated at the SAC's table. Bob informed me that his friend would introduce me to the SAC, which would give me an opportunity to, as Bob said, "strut your stuff." I had a great time and an excellent conversation with the SAC and was feeling good about my chances.

It wasn't until February 03, 1987, that I received a call from FBI Headquarters stating that I had qualified for training. I felt my heart soar. Finally, my time had come! But then they dropped the bomb. I had to start six days later on February 09, 1987.

Without hesitation, I said yes. When I hung up the telephone, I realized I had less than a week before I had to leave for Quantico. I was ecstatic. My dream had come true. It was time for me to prove to myself and my young family that I was meant to be an FBI Special Agent. This is what I had been waiting for ever since I started watching Efrem Zimbalist Jr. as Inspector Erskine. I felt euphoric yet apprehensive. What if I didn't have what it took to be an FBI Special Agent? But then I realized I prepared my whole life for this. This was my dream. There was no way I was going to fail. My desire, work ethic, and upbringing would get me through this. I could not wait to get started.

CHAPTER

7

February 09, 1987

I arrived at the FBI Academy in Quantico, Virginia, anxious to take on what I perceived to be my greatest challenge, and if successful, would lead me to my greatest achievement. I Entered on Duty ("EOD") as a Special Agent of the Federal Bureau of Investigation, ready for my first day of 12 weeks of rigorous training at the FBI Academy at Quantico, VA. I cannot begin to explain how excited yet terrified I was that day. I left my family behind in hopes that my dream would come to fruition because there are no guarantees that you will become an FBI Agent just because you made it to the FBI Academy.

Our class had several fellow new agents dismissed on our third day at the academy. Their hopes and dreams of becoming an FBI Agent shattered. We lost a few more throughout our twelve weeks for failing to pass a required course of instruction or firearms or the physical fitness test.

Watching the dismissal of the other agents terrified me.

The idea that I could fail and be sent home to my family with no job was quite harrowing but also motivating. I did not want to, nor could I afford to let my family down.

We were housed at the FBI Academy in Quantico, VA, which is an all-inclusive facility. The academy occupies 547 acres within Marine Corps Base Quantico. The academy has several buildings, that include dormitories, classrooms, an auditorium, a library, a cafeteria, a gym, and Olympic size pool, locker rooms, firearms ranges, and firearms cleaning and storage room. It is also home to Hogan's Alley, a training complex simulating a small town, Tactical and Emergency Vehicle Operations Center, television viewing rooms, and a bar.

An intense excitement fell over me as I drove onto the FBI Academy grounds and looked at the buildings and the scenery - I actually did it. I was going to be an FBI agent. After I parked my car, I walked across the parking lot, carrying my bags that my wife had packed the night before. I was very nervous as I entered, but nerves were soon overtaken with enthusiasm as each counselor, supervisor, and the other trainees began to gather inside the lobby. They inundated us with identification badges, paperwork, schedules, and room assignments. They even provided us with our clothing.

As I began to meet the other recruits, I was amazed by the various backgrounds and work experience they possessed. It seemed as though people came from all over the country. I met Dennis Allen, a dentist from Detroit, Michigan. Kenny Porter, whose father was an FBI Agent that was killed in the line of duty from Phoenix, Arizona. John Terry, a police officer from Philadelphia, Pennsylvania. Ed

Daer and Matt Valles were from Pittsburg and were a part of the FBI's New Agents Class (NAC 87-7). We were all there for one reason: to become a Special Agent for the FBI. Yet none of us knew what lay ahead.

Supervisory Special Agents from the field were selected to serve each class as New Agent's class supervisor, and a rotating pair of special agents from the field were selected to serve as field counselors.

The class supervisor and the class counselors were significant in the development of each new agent trainee. Our class counselors were our biggest fans and supporters. Like us, they also were away from their families and their field office of assignment.

The counselors took us on our first tour of the academy. I was amazed at everything it had to offer; two dormitories, dozens of classrooms, gymnasium, pool, library, cafeteria, auditorium, and of course, the firearms ranges. It was all quite overwhelming. I loved the facilities and was still amazed that I was here. This was what I had been pursuing since I was a kid. And it was better than I ever dreamed it would be. Tomorrow was going to be the first day of realizing my dream. But to do so, I would have to perform at a level I had yet to reach before.

I was positive that this would be extremely difficult as they only wanted the best of the best. At least that is what they kept telling us. The training would involve academics, which included the basics of the law, ethics, report writing, communications, interviewing, behavioral science, and the various criminal violations that we would be responsible for investigating in the future. Criminal violations such as white-collar crime, organized crime, violent crime, and domestic terrorism.

We would be tested in all these areas, and the one that frightened most of us, except for the lawyers in our class, was the legal exam. I remember hearing about how difficult that exam was on the very first day. Fortunately, we had a great instructor who also had a great sense of humor. He kept things light, but no matter how much we laughed, it was still legal and an important component of our learning process. I still do not understand "curtilage," but fortunately, each field office had their own Chief Legal Counsel assigned to the division who would be more than happy to explain what curtilage is.

I thoroughly enjoyed our time in the classroom. The instructors have experienced agents from the various field offices who brought their particular area of expertise to Quantico. They brought real-life issues, and situations with them, and that brought a unique quality that certainly made a significant impact on me.

Physical fitness was also a significant component of the curriculum at the FBI Academy. On the very first day, we were required to pass the Physical Fitness test. The FBI's test focuses on three areas, and they are; strength, stamina, and speed. The FBI's physical fitness test has very high standards because the duties and responsibilities of an FBI Special Agent are unforgiving when it comes to daily demands and high-intensity situations. It was made very clear that if you respect what the position of being an FBI Special Agent brings, then you must prove yourself by passing this test and maintaining that level of fitness throughout your career.

There were a few who did not attain a minimum passing

score of 15. I believe we lost a few of our classmates that day, and a few others, in addition to their requisite workload, were required to take additional physical fitness training over the next few weeks and were tested at that time to ensure they passed. If any of them failed, they too were sent home.

Throughout our time at the academy, physical fitness training was almost a daily occurrence. It was demanding and challenging, and at the end of each session, I was exhausted. The instructors were unrelenting and continued to push us beyond what we thought we were capable of accomplishing. They did it for a reason; their goal was to ensure that when we left, we were as prepared physically as we were mentally. The instructors knew and understood the physical challenges that we would ultimately be facing.

Defensive tactics were also an essential part of our physical fitness training, and we were taught the different techniques in handcuffing, control holds, boxing, searching subjects, weapon retention, and disarming our would-be assailants. All skills that were necessary to prepare us for when we hit the streets.

The FBI boasts a resolute firearms training program, which has evolved through the years to keep pace with technology and best prepare agents for the ever-increasing dangers and threats they face carrying out their assignments.

The mission of the FBI's firearms training program was to develop and deliver a comprehensive and consistent firearms training curriculum that provided us new agent trainees and special agents the skills needed to safely and effectively use firearms while performing our duties.

The FBI Academy's Firearms training included our

Bureau issued handgun, shotgun, and semi-automatic shoulder weapons. The FBI's Firearm Instructors were and still are some of the best in the world, and their focus was on safety, marksmanship, an acclimation to most of the weapons in the FBI's arsenal, live-fire training, and practical shooting techniques.

We didn't just shoot at stationary targets. We also did combat shooting, close-quarters shooting, shooting weak hand, assault weapons, shotgun, and more. It was as comprehensive as the training I had received with the U.S. Secret Service. One of the techniques our firearms instructor taught us was to practice dry firing our practice weapons in front of a mirror. Our practice weapons were guns without a firing pin, and ammunition could not be placed in the chamber. At this time, the FBI's handgun of choice was the Smith and Wesson Six Shot Revolver.

We also trained on the FATS machine, a firearms training simulation program. The FATS worked like this; in a darkened room, you faced a movie screen with a video simulating a potential crime unfolding. You were there, and you had to decide whether to shoot or not shoot as the scenario played out before you in real-time. If you acted too quickly or misread the situation, you could kill an innocent bystander or possibly your partner. Hesitate, and you could end up becoming the shooting victim. The FATS machine put to shame all of today's computer games. It was awesome and an outstanding way to learn from real-life situations without real-life consequences.

Our training also included defensive driving and surveillance techniques. I likened all the practice and the time we were together to the atmosphere of football camp. You're with this group day in and day out. You eat together, sleep together, study together, socialize together, and train together. The training is grueling, and through the hard work and sacrifices, I started to build friendships and relationships that lasted a lifetime. You depend on one another to help get you through these next four months.

No agent training would be complete without the real-life practicum. The agency sets up criminal scenarios involving bad guys and FBI agents. The characters are all actors following scripts of crimes we may encounter. Whether it is a bank robbery, white-collar crime, or violent crime, these scenarios were designed to enhance an agents' skill set, so they are ready to hit the street running.

The scenarios were taken from real-life cases and integrated into a realistic training exercise. This exercise enhanced our interviewing techniques, evidence collection capabilities. I taught us how to correctly fill out our FD-302s (an official FBI form designed to reflect the results of an agent's interview). We had to work these scenarios as if it was a real crime scene. This was, by far, my favorite part of the training.

About mid-way through our training, we were to receive our Orders of Transfer. Every one of us was anticipating this day. We had made it through some of the most difficult exams and tests and looked forward to finding where we would be working.

Our entire class sat pensively in our seats in the classroom. We would individually get called to the front of the class. Once there, we were to state where we would like to be assigned and where we thought we would be assigned.

"Ray Morrow," Ford Cole, our class counselor, called out.

I walked anxiously to the front of the class. I stated confidently, "I would like to be assigned to the Pittsburgh Field Office, but I am positive that will not be the case, and therefore, I will most probably end up in Divorce Court."

Several people in the room chuckled. When I opened the envelope and read Louisville, KY, Ford Cole stated, "Well, you're not going to Pittsburgh, but hopefully Louisville, Kentucky is close enough to keep you out of court."

I knew nothing about Louisville but was thrilled not to be sent to New York or Los Angeles. Plus, it was only a six-hour drive from Pittsburgh. Hopefully, that would be tolerable for Lynn.

As soon as we finished and everyone had their new office assignments, I immediately called home.

"Louisville," she said as if she was saying, "please kill me now. "How far is that from home?"

I responded immediately, "390 miles approximately a six-hour drive. It will be great, I promise." One of the agents in my class was from Louisville and had nothing but great things to say about it. He also provided great insights into where I should live and what Louisville had to offer. I relayed all that information to Lynn with great enthusiasm. She acknowledged with much suspicion. She knew me so well.

CHAPTER

8

At my graduation ceremony, I received my credentials and my FBI badge by Assistant Director Oliver "Buck" Revell. I held the shiny gold badge in my hand and ran my fingers over the blue F-B-I. I had made it. I was an FBI agent. I was really here. I had to hold back a tear, Inspector Erskine would never have cried on the job, and neither would I. I tucked my credentials and badge into my suit coat pocket. My wife Lynn and son Ross made it to the ceremony, and I was extremely proud when I displayed my badge and credentials to them, yet there was one person missing. I really wished my father could have been there. He would have been so proud, especially when I was awarded the Top Gun award for having the highest overall Firearms score in our class. As we were departing, I held my credentials and badge toward the sky, "This one is for you, dad."

I was ready for duty. I reported for my first day as an FBI agent on May 09, 1987, at FBI's Louisville Field Office. I was introduced to my training agent Walt Jones. Walt had been an FBI Special Agent for close to twenty years. Walt loved the Bureau and had accomplished quite a bit in his time. Walt was gregarious yet steadfast when it came to following the policies, procedures, rules, regulations, and the law. However, he always had an amusing way of showing his adherence to those policies, procedures, rules, regulations, and the law.

"If you ever are unsure, refer to the FBI's Manual of Investigative Operations Guidelines ("MIOGs") and Manual of Administrative Procedures ("MAOP") for guidance. Always," Walt told this to all Agents, new on the job or not.

Special Agent in Charge of the Louisville Field Office, Joel Carlson assigned me to the drug squad, one of the busiest squads in the division. Because I was extremely proficient with firearms and tactical response, I was selected to be a member of the Louisville Division's SWAT team.

The Division's Assistant Special Agent in Charge ("ASAC") Marty Ford supervised both the Drug and Organized Crime squads. Marty was in his early fifties and looked it, although he did his best to maintain a youthfulness with his dress and died black hair that was always well-coiffed. Marty was also well versed in FBI policies and procedures and extremely knowledgeable of the FBI's investigative responsibilities. Marty had a quick wit and always put those of us around him at ease with his easy-going manner.

There were nine total agents in our squad. Jim Insco and John Moran were the two-division pilots on the team. They were responsible for conducting any air surveillance or transportation required by an on-going investigation. Larry Cannel and Tom Nunemaker were young, aggressive first office agents who I typically worked alongside. There were three more senior agents on the team as well. ASAC Marty Ford and I rounded out the squad.

Walt worked with me daily, assisting me with every aspect of my investigative caseload. Walt taught me how to correctly write an FD-302, the FBI's official record of interview. Walt ensured I follow the policy on working informants and cooperating witnesses, as well as conducting interviews. Walt would say, "Most agents get in trouble because of the way they handle their informants. Always keep them at arm's length and never put your complete trust in them. Do it by the book and always have another agent with you when meeting with your informants." I didn't realize at the time how critical that piece of advice would be in my career.

Walt made sure I did everything by the book. He taught me the ins and outs of law enforcement and how to work with the United States Attorney's Office and other various local, state, and federal agencies.

While I was absorbing everything that Walt and my fellow squad agents were teaching me, Lynn, Ross, and Blake were getting acquainted with our new home. At first, Lynn stayed at home to ensure we got the boys settled. Ross was starting first grade, and Blake enrolled in Preschool. After a few months, Lynn was satisfied that she and the boys had their routine down, she started to work at Delta Airlines as a ticket and gate agent at the Louisville International Airport.

July 1987

I had been in the Louisville Division approximately three months when I was called into our ASAC Marty Ford's office.

"Ray, sit down," Mr. Ford said, as I entered his office. There is also a level of respect given to agents of a certain level, such as Marty Ford.

I sat in the seat that Mr. Ford motioned to, and he shut the door behind me. A bubble formed in the back of my throat. I had no idea why I was called in. "Ray, you have been doing a great job, and the boss and I are very impressed with how quickly you pick things up and how well you have adjusted to the office."

I quickly swallowed the bubble and pulled my shoulders back as Mr. Ford continued, "There is a new task force being established that involves several federal agencies and the Kentucky State Police ("KSP"). The task force will focus on domestic marijuana investigations targeting a group of growers and distributors located in Marion County, Kentucky. This is an extremely significant initiative, and we want to be a part of it. The boss and I thought you would be perfect for this."

My head started to swell from all the praise and the consideration of this very significant undertaking. Mr. Ford continued about how important this was to the office, and he was sure he had picked the right agent for this assignment.

"Your first meeting is this morning. Walt will take you to the task force and introduce you to your new team." Mr. Ford stuck his head out the door and called for Walt to come into the office.

80

I was speechless. I had only been on the job for a few months. I was sure this had to signify how well I was doing. I couldn't wait to go home and tell Lynn about this development!

Mr. Ford informed Walt that I had just been briefed on my new assignment and that we should head to this task force's first meeting as soon as possible.

Walt and I headed to the meeting in Walt's brand new four-door Plymouth. Now, I felt important because Walt never drove when we went out, he always made me drive. He said it was so I could learn the area, but the rumor was Walt just liked being chauffeured around. As we headed to the meeting at the local KSP office, Walt said to me, "Do you know what this is all about?"

"Marty told me it was a task force focused on a group of marijuana growers based in Marion County," I replied.

Walt chuckled, "Yes, but did Marty tell you why you were selected?"

I informed Walt of all the accolades Marty had laid on me when we were in the office before, he had called Walt in. Walt's chuckle turned into a full-blown laugh. I was puzzled. I was missing the punchline. "That is not exactly why you were selected. You see, about a year ago, the DEA and the KSP were working a big drug investigation, and just before they were about to break it open, we got involved without notifying them and sort of stole the case. Both the DEA and KSP were very upset there hasn't been much communication between them and us, and they are refusing to work with us. They hate us."

The bubble returned in my throat. And it was growing fast.

"We were not invited to be a part of this task force, but FBIHQ wants us to be involved as we are one of only three states given the authority to work these types of investigations. So, we all thought since you're so new, they can't hate you too much, and that's how you were selected for this assignment," Walt continued, as my anxiety grew.

Just then, we pulled into the parking lot of the one-story building located just outside the city limits of Louisville. My head shrunk significantly, my ego deflated, and my anxiety was at an all-time high as I walked towards the room full of very hostile people who did not want me there.

I followed Walt into the office, and we walked down a hallway to a large conference room where the meeting was just about to start. All of the participants, John Krawczyk from the IRS, Rick Sanders, and Rich Badaracco from the DEA, a Captain, Lieutenant, and Sergeant from the KSP, were all seated in a semi-circle around the Assistant United States Attorney, David Grice. AUSA Grice was leading this group. As Walt and I walked into the room, all eyes turned towards us, and if looks could kill, we would have been long gone. There was plenty of the crossing of arms, the rolling of the eyes was very apparent, and a lot of grunts and groans of obvious disgust as we walked in. They made no qualms in letting us know that we were not welcome. There were two seats left at the end of the semi-circle, and Walt sat next to DEA Agent, Rick Sanders, and I took the last seat.

David Grice opened the meeting, "Welcome everyone.

How about we start by going around the room and introducing ourselves?" He started the introductions at the end opposite of where Walt and I were sitting. Each participant gave their name and what agency they represented. It was finally Walt's turn. He stood up and cleared his throat, "I'm Walt Jones with the FBI, and if you play ball with us, we'll shove the bat right up your ass."

I nearly choked on my spit. Dumfounded, I could not believe Walt had just said that. *How am I going to work with these guys now?* The room was silent for a moment that seemed to linger on for eternity. My head was ringing. I tried to gather strength in my knees to stand for my introduction, but before I could, Walt started laughing, and everyone followed suit. It took me a moment, as it did everyone else, to realize that this was Walt's way of apologizing and accepting responsibility for the FBI's past behavior. With that, I was able to introduce myself to a much friendlier crowd.

Grice began to go into detail on the investigation, explaining that we were targeting a group of marijuana growers and distributors based in Marion County, Kentucky referred to as The Cornbread Mafia.

This was the initial meeting and the beginning of this task force effort that would run for over two years. As part of this task force, I was involved in every aspect of the investigation. We conducted numerous surveillance tactics, interviews, search warrants, arrests, traveled to nine different states, and seized the property and marijuana we located on each farm. Most of my days were spent working this case. However, not all. There was always something new thrown into my case-load to mix things up.

A few weeks after starting my new assignment on the

task force, I was sent out to Pikeville, Kentucky. Pikeville was a small two-man Resident Agency located in Eastern Kentucky. I was in Pikeville to cover some leads on a drug investigation and had a few names and addresses of those I needed to interview. Pikeville is a tiny, close-knit town mining town, and cooperation with law enforcement at best would be minimal, and I knew it.

I headed for my first interview. I had the address, but back then, there was no GPS. Although, I'm still not convinced it would have covered some of these addresses. As I drove to my first interview, I rehearsed what I was going to say. I was half expecting to break this case wide open with my first interview. I figured it was still early in the day, and that I could be home by tonight if I did this right.

I drove for what seemed like hours and just could not find my first address. I knew I was driving in circles as I kept passing this one little gas station on the corner. Finally, I stopped at the gas station to ask for directions. I went inside and asked the attendant if he could help me find this address. He looked at the paper I handed to him with the address and then asked me to follow him outside.

When we got out, he provided me with these directions. "You go to the second holler. Then go past the third yardcar on your right and make a right follow that road all the way down to the end, you can't miss it."

I was even more confused now then I was before. What the hell was a holler and a yardcar? "I just have a few questions."

"Shoot," he said, sucking on his toothpick.

"What's a holler?" He looked at me like I was from Mars or something.

"Son, do you see the top of that hill over there?" he asked.

I nodded. "When you get to the top of that hill, you drive all the way down to the bottom. Now you're in a holler."

"So, the very bottom of the hill is a holler?"

"Yes."

"One more question. What's a yardcar?"

Again, I got a look, and the response was, "Son, that's a car sitting in the yard."

"What if the car has been moved?"

The man laughed, "Son, that car will be there, it ain't been moved, and it ain't gonna be moved."

I knew right then I had better leave well enough alone and just move on with these directions. I thanked him and went on my way. I drove up to the top of the hill and then to the bottom. That's one holler down, I thought to myself. I did the same at the next hill. Now I just need to identify and count three yardcars. I drove on, and there they were. First one, then a short time later the second and then there it was the third yardcar. I went on just a short distance, and there was my right-hand turn just like he said. I followed this so-called road a short distance, and there it was a trailer with a huge satellite dish on the side.

I gathered my stuff and went to the door and knocked. A reasonably large man in bib overalls came to the door. I pulled out my FBI credentials displayed them for this large gentleman to see then I introduced myself as Special Agent Ray A. Morrow. "Can I ask you a few questions?"

This large man looked at my credentials, looked at me, and then said to me, "Mr. Morrow, I appreciate who you are and what you do, but you can just go fuck yourself."

I was stunned. This never happened at Quantico. Why didn't they teach us this at Quantico? What do I do now? This can't be happening. How can he not answer my questions? He started to walk back towards his front door, and I called out to him, "Sir, I don't think you heard me."

"I heard you. Maybe you didn't hear me?" And with that, he walked back into his home.

I was flabbergasted and extremely disillusioned. How could this be? When I reported back to the Pikeville Resident Agency, I found out this was quite a common theme here in Pikeville. I breathed a huge sigh of relief, knowing that my FBI career would not be short-lived.

A few weeks later, it was early Monday morning when I arrived at the office, and Special Agent John Moran was waiting for me in the lobby. John said, "We have to head out to a location where Tom (Nunemaker) and Larry (Cannel) are with two drug dealers they have been working with all weekend cooking meth they want us to come out to where they are to make the arrests." Yes, this is a great way to start the week!

We got back in my car and started. John stated that we needed to get there as soon as possible as the two bad guys were high after cooking meth all weekend. It had been raining most of the night and was still raining when we headed out. It was approximately 6:30 am, and there was very little traffic at the time. Based on the wet road conditions, I was going faster than I should have, but John kept saying we needed to get there as soon as possible as neither Tom nor Larry had their weapons with them.

We were on a four-lane divided highway moving along at a pretty good clip when the car started to hydroplane. I

86

had never unintentionally hydroplaned before, but I immediately started to react the way they taught me at the FBI Academy and back when I attended the U.S. Secret Service Training Academy. My reactions took over as the car spun several times, and all I saw were various things flashing in front of me. We never crossed the center line, and fortunately, there was no other traffic on our side of the road. Finally, for what seemed like an eternity, the car straightened out, and we were facing in the right direction.

I gathered myself and tried not to show John that I was terrified. I must have hidden the look of fear because John said, "Wow, that was amazing."

"I have no idea how I did that," I said, vomiting the truth. We finally arrived safely at the location, and as John and I got out of the car. Tom came out of the house and walked towards us. "The two mopes are sitting on the couch to your right when you enter, and Larry is in the kitchen straight ahead."

John and I ran up to and through the front door, guns were drawn. I was in a full sprint and entered the house first. The two suspects were sitting on the couch. John was right behind me. But just then to my left out of the corner of my eye, I saw movement and someone standing in a small room. I looked to the left and was ready to charge. I took one step, and the next thing I knew, I was staring at the ceiling. My head cracked down hard on the linoleum floor. Ouch! I had slipped on a little throw rug and went flying. From the ground, I yell, "Put your hands up and don't move." John was yelling the same thing. The two on the couch sat there in stunned silence, hands in the air.

I jumped up, gave my head a rub, and walked towards

the sofa. John was already there and had the two under control. I looked to my left, and there stood Rick Sanders of the DEA. I was so embarrassed. Anyway, we made the arrests, and my acrobatic entrance was the talk of the office for quite some time.

Spring 1988

SWAT was one of my favorite duties while in Louisville. I knew whenever a case was assigned that something exciting was bound to happen. So, when I walked into the office that April morning, a rush came over me when my SWAT team Leader, Mike Phillips, and ASAC Ford called us all into the briefing room.

Two prisoners had escaped from one of the local County Detention Centers the previous night. ASAC Ford stated, "They killed a prison guard and wounded two others before their escape. We got word they were spotted in Louisville and that they are armed and extremely dangerous," Ford said, his tone as serious as I have ever heard it.

Phillips put the photos of the two escapees on the board. The one guy was your typical thug. Tattoos up and down his arms and neck. He had to weigh a good 300 pounds and could have easily tossed my slender 5'10" frame across the room. The other guy was prematurely balding and was on the skinny side, except for his bloated belly. Both men were serving time for murder.

"The two individuals were last seen driving a blue Ford Taurus, license plate number XVJ-184. An informant told us that they would be traveling only at night and are trying to make their way to a house in Jeffersontown, Kentucky."

The attack plan was known as the Tactical Vehicle Intervention (TVI). A TVI is a pursuit tactic utilized by law enforcement when in pursuit of a fleeing vehicle, which can force the fleeing suspect's vehicle to turn sideways abruptly, causing the driver to lose control and stop. The plan was to prevent them from getting back to their planned location, which we were informed had a significant number of weapons and ammunition.

I was going to ride with Special Agent Larry Cannel, who would be driving the ramming vehicle that would hit the suspects' car. I would be in the back seat, and my job, when Larry rammed the car, was to, if necessary, take the driver out first and then the passenger next with a shotgun. A rush of adrenaline flowed through my veins. This would be my first car chase.

"You will be less than one foot from the driver, and when we ram them, if it's done right, our cars will be up against one another, and you should be facing them," Larry explained.

I got a little nervous when I heard that. But for some ungodly reason, I was excited to take on this task. We waited until around 1:00 am and found out from our informant (who was a friend of the suspects but was more than willing to give them up for a hefty payday from the FBI) that they never left their residence. We had spent approximately six hours in our vehicle, waiting and preparing for the capture.

The next night we were informed they were staying at a local motel. We went to the motel, which was located just outside of Louisville, and confirmed they were there. Mike

Phillips approached the night desk clerk. "You the guy in charge tonight?" he asked the wiry young man.

"I am the manager on duty," the kid replied, his voice shaky.

Phillips pulled out his badge, "we need your help."

The kid's eyes grew wide as Phillips explained the situation. Phillips asked the kid to contact every room occupied by a guest, other than the suspects, and tell them to leave their room quietly and come to the front desk. Fortunately, there were only a few rooms occupied that evening.

As the guests quickly and quietly departed the rooms, the SWAT team headed to the back parking lot to go over each step of our response plan. We had rehearsed over and over until the call came that all guests had been relocated. We then got into our positions and lined up outside the room of the suspects. Larry carried a sledgehammer. It was his job to bust open the door on command, then step aside and let the agents behind him rush the room. There were also four SWAT members standing to the side of the large front window of the room. Their instructions were to bust the window, move the curtains, and shine flashlights into the room. Two SWAT members stood outside the small bathroom window in the back of the hotel to make sure they didn't try to exit through that window. Mike gave Larry the 'go' sign. Larry busted open the door with his sledgehammer. Within a matter of seconds, we entered the room expeditiously and matter-of-factly subdued and handcuffed the prisoners before they knew what hit them.

CHAPTER

October 1988

I arrived at 0600 hours, as usual. Typically, it was all quiet on the front first thing in the morning. I liked arriving earlier than the rest of my team so I could get my paperwork done in peace. But today, the floor was already in full swing. Our new ASAC Tom Miller and SWAT Leader Mike Phillips had papers sprawled out on the conference table. Something was up.

Phillips caught my eye as I walked by the glass door. "Morrow, have the entire team come to the conference room soon as they arrive."

I gave a quick salute to acknowledge and confirm. By 0700, the entire team had gathered around the table, coffee in hand.

"We have information that a three-man professional hit team is on their way to Lexington to kill a local drug dealer who had ripped off a drug cartel out of the Dominican Republic," Phillips announced.

"How do we know this?" Larry asked.

Phillips and Miller started to laugh, "Ironically, the idiot drug dealer came to us for protection," Miller said.

"What's the deal?" I asked.

Miller explained that this three-person hit team was from the Dominican Republic and unfamiliar with the area. They had put the word out in their network that they needed someone to assist them in locating the local drug dealer and scouting out the area. Our informant was able to make contact and then introduce our undercover agent to the hit team as someone who both knew their target and the area and could arrange to set up their target for a price.

After our undercover agents' initial meeting, it was determined by our legal team that we would need to catch this hit team in the act. Thus, it was not going to be as simple as grabbing the guys before they attacked. The undercover agent and the informant continued to appear as though they were working with the hit team to locate their target. The rest of our team worked on how and where to set up the hitmen best.

Jim Huggins, the Supervisory Special Resident Agent in Charge of the Lexington Resident Agency ("RA"), approached the motel owner and made the arrangements for us to use the motel to intercept this three-man hit team. We spent several days running through every scenario. We checked every door, window, stairway. These guys were out for blood, and they wouldn't care if they took down a few FBI agents along the way. We couldn't be too careful.

Mike Phillips firmly believed that preparation and practice readied us for the real thing. It allowed us to react instantly in extraordinarily stressful situations, and that preparation allowed us to adjust immediately to any problem that may arise.

Finally, we were all set. The undercover agent met one last time with the hit team and informed them that their target would be at the motel on the following day. That morning we met with our ASAC Tom Miller and Mike Phillips and were briefed one last time on our assignments. The SWAT team, with air support from our pilots, were ready.

Our SWAT team moved to the predetermined location and again rehearsed the scenario numerous times. The hotel had cleared of all guests, and all hotel employees were replaced with FBI agents.

"The targets are on the way to your location," came across our radios. We were in place. Waiting. Ready. The voice came again, "They have stopped at a local K-Mart. We will alert when they leave." We paused, waiting for the next move.

The call came again from our pilots, "The hit team had departed K-mart and is again en route to the hotel."

Our SWAT Supervisor radioed for two agents to go to K-Mart to see if they could determine what the hit team had purchased. We knew the group was heavily armed, and they were coming to the motel to meet their target. We didn't know if they would kill their mark at the motel or take him to a more remote area. Because of this, we planned to make sure they did not leave the motel.

The plan called for the hitmen to meet with our informant, who would then introduce them to the motel's front desk clerk (an undercover agent). The agent would provide them with the key to the room of the target. The informant told the hit team that the desk clerk was a good friend who could be trusted. By having the key, they could quickly enter the room and surprise and easily subdue their target.

Our pilots continued to call out the exact whereabouts of the hit team's vehicle until they finally arrived. The two agents that went to K-mart radioed that the hit team had purchased duct tape, rope, and shovels. It appeared to us they were going to take their subject hostage, torture, kill, and then bury him.

"One member of the team has exited the vehicle and is heading towards the front desk," the pilots announced over the radio.

The man entered the motel lobby, where the undercover agent greeted him. The agent handed the hitman a key without a word. A moment later, the hitman was back outside and got back into the car. He drove around to the back of the motel, closer to the room where their subject was located. The vehicle pulled into a parking spot. We heard the call from our pilots, "Car is parked. No one has exited the vehicle."

Anticipation began to boil inside me. We began to move slowly. A few members of the SWAT team began to pull into place, waiting for the hitmen to make it to the room before blocking both exits with a vehicle barricade. SWAT members were inside all the surrounding rooms, along with every foreseeable exit and vantage point. There was complete silence. More than three minutes had passed, and the men remained in their car. My mind was racing, and patience was running thin. *Why the hell won't they get out of the car!*?

Finally, the pilots called out, "Two members of the team are making their way towards the door. A third remains in the vehicle, driver's seat."

The two men were large and very scary looking. They would have been scary looking even if they weren't armed with automatic shoulder weapons and pistols, but they were. I could hear my heart pounding. The call came from our pilots, "they are at the door."

We moved like the wind to get into position. As the hitman fumbled with the key, the two doors on either side of the target's room swung open, and like a swarm of bees, we surrounded the two men.

"Drop your weapons," Phillips yelled.

They didn't. The hitmen began to fire their weapons. Dozens of rounds flew between both the hit team and SWAT. The two individuals at the door fell to the ground immediately. One was dead, the other severely wounded. The man who remained in the car attempted to flee the scene. He was shot in the back before he reached the barricade. No FBI agents were injured.

Those 15-20 seconds and the immediate aftermath of the takedown were some of the most intense in my life. That was the first time I saw anyone die. Their faces are etched in my mind forever.

March 1989

I was two months from my second anniversary in the Louisville FBI Filed Office, and with that, the Cornbread Mafia case was also coming to an end. It had been a wild ride. We had apprehended and prosecuted 73 individuals and confiscated over 192 tons of marijuana, worth over $350 million, from twenty-nine different farms located in nine different states.

With all that I knew, my time in Louisville would be coming to an end, and I was positive like all of the first office agents before me I would be packing up and heading to the New York Field Office. At that time, that was every first office agent's nightmare.

CHAPTER

April 1989

While still assigned to the FBI Louisville Division, I applied to the Primary Undercover Agent in a Police Corruption investigation in Cleveland, Ohio.

Lynn was not aware that I had done this, and I was not sure how I was going to explain it to her if I was selected. But then again, there was no way they were going to choose me as I had no undercover experience. But I figured, what the heck, right?

During my first six months in the Louisville Division, I read *Donnie Brasco*, by former FBI Agent Joseph D. Pistone. Before reading the book, I had never considered doing undercover work. Still, after reading Joe Pistone's book, I became fascinated with the thought of pursuing an opportunity to work undercover in the FBI.

Throughout the book, Mr. Pistone detailed what it took to make it as an undercover agent. He explained that even if you did everything right, there were no guarantees that it would all work out. Mr. Pistone described in detail the harrowing situations he found himself in and how he was able to come out of it relatively unscathed. Mr. Pistone was a real-life Inspector Erskine and more. Now, I wanted to be Donnie Brasco.

At this point, I had never met Joe Pistone. But now, after reading his book, I surely wanted to test myself to see if I could measure up. However, after reading what Joe and his family had been through, I was still not quite sure why I would want to put my family and me through something like that. Although, I must admit that my fascination with *Donnie Brasco* was not the only reason I wanted to pursue an undercover position in Cleveland, Ohio.

At the time, the FBI had a Top 12 program. I was trying to avoid it. What that meant was all first office agents leaving the academy were assigned to an FBI Field Office. There were three types of FBI field offices, Small, Medium, and Large. Small field offices like Columbia, South Carolina, or Birmingham, Alabama. Medium field offices included field offices such as Pittsburgh, Pennsylvania, Milwaukee, Wisconsin, or Tampa, Florida. And then there were the Top Twelve Large Field Offices, which were: New York City, Detroit, Chicago, Los Angeles, San Francisco, Boston, Washington D.C., Philadelphia, Miami, Cleveland, Baltimore, and Newark.

Typically, first office agents that were initially assigned to a large field office stayed there for at least six years. If they then decided they wanted to pursue a career in management, they could start applying for supervisory positions. If they choose to leave after the six years, they could put in for an Office of Preference ("OP"). It usually took much longer than six years to get an OP.

First office agents were sent to a small or medium-sized field office that would typically transfer to one of the FBI's Top 12 after three years. During my time in Louisville, almost every first office agent ended up being sent to New York, the most dreaded of the Top 12. I did not want to go to New York but was sure that I would most likely end up there. And I was terrified of how Lynn would feel about this move.

So, as my second year in the Louisville Division was beginning, I was thinking more and more about how I would avoid the move to New York. As other agents got their transfer orders to New York, I began to hear the horror stories of the cost of living and the ungodly commutes they would be facing. Some new agents simply resigned from the FBI rather than move their families to New York. The idea of moving to New York bothered me, but I would never discuss this with Lynn. I was positive that she would have me resign for the sake of our family, and I knew I would never resign from the FBI.

I always made it known to my fellow squad agents that I would love to get Cleveland, Ohio, as my Top 12 assignment. Not that it would ever happen, but I thought if I told enough people maybe just maybe someone would grant my wish.

However, there was one agent from the Louisville Division who did get assigned to the Cleveland FBI Field Office, and that was Dan Estrem. Dan was selected because he was one helluva case agent and was even better at identifying, developing, and utilizing confidential informants.

Before Dan departed for Cleveland, I reminded him how

much I wanted to be assigned to Cleveland as well when my time was up here in Louisville. Just in case he was able to help in any way he could.

Dan left before my second year in Louisville was up. I hadn't spoken to Dan since he left. But Tom Nunemaker informed me that Dan was initiating a Group I Undercover Operation ("UCO") and was looking for a primary undercover agent.

A Group 1 UCO is an extremely sensitive and significant investigation that utilizes the undercover technique, usually with a trained and certified undercover agent. These types of investigations must be approved by FBI Headquarters (FBIHQ) and the Department of Justice (DOJ). They usually are funded, and run-in six-month increments, and the funding is routinely in the hundreds of thousands of dollars. The targets of these investigations are typically high-value targets. These Group 1 undercover operations are closely monitored and intensely scrutinized and must strictly adhere to The Attorney General's (AGs) Guidelines on FBI Undercover Operations, as well as all of the FBI's policies and procedures and also work within the framework of the law.

The AG Guidelines provide instructions on the proper use of undercover techniques, which are essential to the detection, prevention, and prosecution of white-collar crimes, public corruption, terrorism, organized crime, offenses involving controlled substances, and other priority areas of investigation.

More importantly, the AG Guidelines provide the FBI with the authority to engage in undercover activities and undercover operations that are appropriate to carry out its law enforcement responsibilities, including the conduct of preliminary inquiries, general crime investigations, and criminal intelligence investigations.

However, these techniques inherently involve an element of deception. They may require cooperation with persons whose motivation and conduct are open to questions and need to be carefully considered and monitored. Therefore, the AG Guidelines are incredibly vital to ensuring the integrity of the investigation.

When a proposed undercover application is approved, there must be careful consideration given regarding the risks and benefits of the operation. And the following factors must be considered and addressed if required:

(1) The risk of personal injury to individuals, property damage, financial loss to persons or businesses, damage to reputation, or other harm to persons;

(2) The risk of civil liability or other loss to the Government;

(3) The risk of invasion of privacy or interference with privileged or confidential relationships and any potential constitutional concerns or other legal concerns;

(4) The risk that individuals engaged in undercover operations may become involved in certain restricted illegal conduct and

(5) The suitability of Government participation in the type of activity that is expected to occur during the operation.

An FBI Undercover Operation allows the undercover agent to get deep inside a criminal organization or entity.

This enables the investigators to identify and document illegal activity fully. This, in turn, provides the prosecutors with firsthand, timely, and more robust evidence and typically directs the investigators and prosecutors to identify the leaders of a particular criminal organization.

An undercover operation, if done correctly, takes you into the inner workings of a criminal organization. It leads you to informants, cooperating witnesses, even consensual monitoring (wiretaps) can't. It will uncover the leaders, the decision-makers, and how they operate. As far as I am concerned, it is the most effective investigative tool a law enforcement agency has in its tool belt.

One other thing to understand is the scrutiny and oversight that is involved in conducting this type of investigation as it is incredibly invasive. Consequently, before initiating an FBI Undercover Operation both the DOJ and the FBI are required to address several risk factors such as; the undercover agent's safety; possible damage to public institutions because of FBI manipulation and interference; injury to a target's reputation; "entrapment" or "outrageous government conduct;" and damage to 3rd parties because of the FBI's generating or creating a crime. So, on top of everything else, numerous concerns need to be identified and addressed before initiating a Group I UCO.

As I was waiting for my turn to get orders to New York, Dan was busy developing informants who were providing information as to the most serious public corruption issue facing the Cleveland Division. Dan, through his informants, determined it was police corruption. Dan received information that members of the Cleveland Police Department were involved in, dealing drugs out of their police cruisers, running bookmaking operations, and protecting illegal gambling operations.

Information from two informants allowed Dan to establish predication on Cleveland Police Sergeant Ron Charles, who was in charge of a Vice squad and Shirley Connor, his associate helping him run his bookmaking operation. Dan received approval from FBIHQ, DOJ, and a judge to operate a couple of Title III wire intercepts. From the information Dan was getting off these Title IIIs, he decided the best way to address this situation was with a Group 1 Undercover Operation. Dan thought by introducing an undercover agent as a gambler who operated an illegal casino. He could get these police officers to shake down the undercover agent.

Through Dan's efforts, the Cleveland Division established a squad to assist Dan with his upcoming undercover operation. Dan identified what type of undercover agent he was looking for and the division's undercover coordinator was given the task of finding Mr. Right.

As the Cleveland Division's Undercover coordinator John Lavoie scoured the FBI for an undercover agent specifically for this assignment, he happened to contact Tom Nunemaker to see if he would be interested in going undercover. Tom had no desire to go to Cleveland but told John that he had someone who would most likely jump at the opportunity. That was me!

Thus, when Tom asked me, I jumped at the chance, especially since it was in Cleveland, and I had just finished reading Donny Brasco for a second time. I was positive that I was more than ready for this assignment. I mean, I just reread Joe's book, of course, I was ready. Although I must admit to you that reading his book made me no more prepared than it did anyone else that turned the pages. Even so, I was willing to believe anything that would get me out of New York. I contacted Dan to let him know that I was interested in the undercover position that he was currently looking to fill. Dan and I spoke for a while about the opportunity. Dan said he would get back to me. After hearing about the position, I was convinced that I would not hear from Dan again. There was no way they would take a chance on a newbie. Boy, was I wrong. A few days later, I did get a call from Dan, along with an invitation to interview for the undercover assignment.

CHAPTER

11

April 1989

The FBI flew me to Cleveland for an in-person interview with Dan Estrem, the squad supervisor Herb Cohrs, Assistant Special Agent in Charge ("ASAC") Larry Collins, and Special Agent in Charge ("SAC") Bill Branon. The interviews lasted all day, and my inexperience in both the FBI and undercover operations came shining through. The only thing I had going for me at this point was my honesty, sincerity, and the undeniable passion, for this undercover operation. I never let them see any self-doubt on my part or gave them any indication that I would not be able to pull this off.

But there was simply no way I could hide the fact that I had no undercover experience and had only been an agent for two years. This was going to be a massive case that targeted the Cleveland Police Department. It also required the agent to run a casino like a skilled gambler. Something I was not. Considering all my shortcomings, I was positive that there was absolutely no way they were going to select me for their undercover operation, especially since their target was police officers. Because who would know an undercover operation better than the police? Wouldn't they be able to spot one a mile away? How in the world would I be able to pull that off?

During my eight hours of interviews, I met with the Division's Undercover Coordinator, John LaVoie. He discussed the Undercover and Sensitive Operations Guidelines as well as the AG Guidelines.

John and Dan explained precisely what they expected from their undercover agent. Dan went over details of the case and the informants involved. Dan wanted someone he could trust and was not a rogue who would do whatever he wanted. Dan expected the undercover agent to be educated on the Undercover Guidelines and FBI policies. Dan demanded loyalty. John wanted someone who had extensive experience in undercover and would, when necessary, buck the system. It was apparent they were not on the same page.

We also talked about running the casino.

"I'm not much of a gambler," I admitted.

"I figured that," Dan said.

I spent a lot of time with Dan, who also introduced me to Special Agent John Ligato, an experienced undercover agent who was assigned to a different squad but was a close friend of Dan's. Dan wanted me to meet with John just to talk about his undercover experience, and John let me know that if I ever needed to speak, he was available. John spoke to me about his past undercover experiences and expressed to me more than once, "It's your ass on the line do what you feel needs to be done. Don't let those who don't have a clue convince you to do something you feel in your gut is wrong."

John and Dan talked about their experience as undercover agents. John had worked several undercover investigations throughout his FBI career that involved drugs and organized crime. When Dan was a police officer, he did a lot of undercover drug work. Dan talked about the case and some of his informants.

We also talked about running a casino, and knowing that I was not much of a gambler, Dan suggested that if I do get selected, they could send me to the FBI Academy to spend some time with some of the FBI's best gamblers. Dan was all business but willing to listen as to why I thought I could do this.

I also met with Herb Cohrs, the Public Corruption Squad's Supervisor, in the Cleveland office. He talked about what his thoughts about the operation were and that this case was important not only to the squad but to the entire Cleveland Division.

Mr. Branon also spoke about his expectations of this undercover operation and how this was not going to be another Operation Corkscrew.

Operation Corkscrew was an undercover operation that had failed miserably and left the Cleveland FBI with a huge black eye. For four years, the FBI Cleveland Office had assigned as many as thirty agents to a case that targeted alleged corruption in the Cleveland Municipal Court System. Of the five convictions obtained in Operation Corkscrew, one was against the FBI's middleman who the FBI had used to set up, what ended up being, phony meetings and phony bribe payments with the judges that weren't judges. Two convictions went against the individuals who fooled the FBI Agents into believing they were judges. In addition, five FBI Agents were disciplined as well.

From April 1980 to April 1981, the undercover agent had twenty-six meetings with seven people he thought were judges while paying thousands of dollars in bribes, to their middleman, that they thought were dealing with the judges. It was not until one of the FBI Agents assigned to the investigation saw one the real judges on television, did he realize they had been duped. The Cleveland FBI was obviously, humiliated and spent the next several months explaining to Congress what exactly went wrong. The Cleveland FBI was extremely cautious this time around and made sure everyone involved in this new case was very aware that this new UCO had to be pristine. They missed on the judges, and now our targets were police officers.

Mr. Cohrs and Mr. Branon both stressed that nothing could go wrong with this investigation as the oversight would be significant. To say I was nervous would be an understatement. I was aware of my lack of experience as I am sure Dan and his team were as well. I did my best to explain all that I had learned during my time in executive protection and how they were very similar.

"An undercover agent, just like an executive protection specialist, must possess three traits; passion, preparation, and perseverance. And while I may lack the firsthand skills of running an undercover operation, I certainly have the necessary traits to pull it off," I said, knowing that it was true.

I went on to explain that an undercover agent must have passion. Passion was required to keep the undercover agent precise and focused. Passion unleashes creativity, which is a significant attribute for an undercover agent. I was confident that without passion, an undercover agent and the project would simply fade away.

Preparation was also required to thoroughly understand the cover story, which had to be formulated and prepared with pristine detail. The undercover agent must be prepared to completely follow the applicable criminal laws and agencies' policies and procedures. The main objective of each meeting or recorded conversation had to be outlined and planned in great detail, attain that objective. It's all about preparation.

But if things don't go as expected, you must be flexible and adaptable. Just like in executive protection. In executive protection, if you have to resort to utilizing your firearm, you have already failed. Your preparation was not good enough. The same goes for an undercover agent; if you fail to prepare, you will inevitably reach a point of last resort.

Lastly, I discussed the necessity of perseverance. It was essential because an undercover operation was a marathon. There would be many highs but also many lows, along with hurdles unexpected hurdles. And the only way to overcome that is to persevere to continue to maintain your focus.

I ended my spiel by telling Dan, "I may not be skilled or experienced, but I promise, you won't find anyone more passionate or determined to get the job done."

As the day of interviewing came to an end, Dan, John, Mr. Cohrs, Mr. Collins, and Mr. Branon sat down with me for a final moment. I assumed they would tell me they would get back to me; that way, they wouldn't have to let me down in person. I was ready for the blow-off. But instead, Dan said, "Welcome to the team."

I could feel the blood rush to my head. *Had I heard that correctly?* I stared at the five men like a deer in headlights. I couldn't believe it I was selected as the Primary Undercover Agent in a police corruption investigation in Cleveland, Ohio. I was ecstatic, overjoyed, delighted, euphoric. The feeling quickly faded as I began to wonder what the hell did I get myself into. *Did I just bite off more than I could chew?* Guess I was about to find out.

"Thank you, sir," I said. "Thank you for your confidence."

Then reality set in. The only way that I was going to be an FBI undercover agent was if I could convince Lynn that this was not just the right opportunity for me but also her and the boys. My mind was ablaze as I headed back to Louisville. I was beyond ecstatic about the opportunity I was just handed. But I realized I had one more hurdle ahead. Lynn. I had to break the news to her. And I had to do it in a way that made her feel at ease. I prepared to address any of her questions or disagreements. I had to persevere and not let her wear me down or back off. I figured if I could get her to buy what I was selling her, then maybe, just maybe I could pull this whole undercover thing off.

Our discussion was lively. Lynn was very concerned about the danger of going up against police officers, and she knew me well enough to know that I was not going to be around as much as I promised. She was concerned about our sons and the fact that they needed their father to be around. I stayed firm in my beliefs and followed my guidelines, and she finally conceded. Although I knew in the back of her mind, she reserved the right to say, "I told you so."

The excitement and anticipation grew daily until it was time to report to my new undercover assignment. Then reality set in.

CHAPTER

May 1989

After being selected, I was sent to Quantico to learn how to gamble. My investigation was going to target illegal gambling and bookmaking operations and the police officers who protected and directed them. Gambling was the centerpiece of my undercover operation, and I had never gambled a day in my life. I didn't understand the lingo. I didn't know how to properly place a bet on a craps table, let alone make the proper payoff. I didn't know if a flush beat three of a kind. I knew absolutely nothing, and I needed to learn fast before I moved to the capital of Rock and Roll.

I landed in Virginia one week before my move to Cleveland. That gave me seven days to learn how to play like a professional gambler. As I made my way towards the massive concrete structure, I began to panic. I was in over my head. I wanted to turn back, swallow my pride, and make my way back to Louisville. But I couldn't. The last thing I wanted was to haul my family to New York City. My choice was undercover in Cleveland or banished to New York.

Lynn was not happy about Cleveland. But she would have been furious about New York. I had to do this. I had to pull it off. I pulled open the massive glass doors to one of the three, seven-story concrete, and glass buildings are known as the dormitories at the FBI Academy in Quantico, Virginia, and made my way to the center of the hall. I stood in the middle of the FBI crest tiled on the floor. I looked up and exhaled deeply. This was my chance.

I went from there to the reception desk and provided my name and FBI Credentials to the FBI employee working at the front desk. I was handed a packet that had my room assignment and a schedule of my activities for the week. Over the next several days, I was to work with several FBI undercover agents who specialized in gambling.

These were some of the FBI's very best gamblers. Each had their area of expertise and very quickly proved to me that they were some of the best undercover gamblers the FBI had to offer. They were to teach me everything I needed to know. And I needed to know a lot. I had never gambled in my life. Not at a table or even on a football game.

"Welcome, Ray," Pete Christ said, his hand out for a shake.

"Hello," I replied, swallowing my nerves.

"You ready to play some cards?" he asked with a wink.

"Ready as I will ever be," I said, not ready at all.

A few of the undercover agents, including Pete, were there from the Cleveland Division. Some others were brought in from other divisions for a few days as well. They all took turns as players and dealers. They took me under their wing. It was like I was a class project for them, and they wanted to get an A. But that is just the way FBI agents are. Always willing to give of themselves to help a fellow agent. Truly remarkable.

My first meeting with these undercover agents was in one of the Academy's classrooms, where each undercover agent introduced themselves and talked about some of the gambling cases, they participated in. I started to feel incompetent and incapable as I listened to them describe their extensive knowledge, skills, and abilities they possessed as gambling experts. I feared I was never going to be able to pull this off.

I listened while Special Agent Pete Christ talked about playing card games and casino gambling in general. Special Agents Vincent Wincelowicz, Herm Groman, and Ed Keller talked about table games. Agent's Christ, Groman, and Keller would be working with me periodically during the Cleveland operation, posing as gamblers at the casino.

My head was spinning as they used gambling terms I had never heard of before, especially regarding craps. Terms like Crap out, Ace Deuce, Apron, House edge, Behind the line, Marker, Come bet, Insurance bet, Off bets, On bets, and so many more. It was as if they were speaking a foreign language, and I needed a quick lesson in Rosetta Stone.

Over the next several days, I met with these agents and others at Hogan's Alley in a room set up like a casino. They had craps tables, poker tables, blackjack tables, almost everything you would find in any casino. Here we would go over all of the little nuances of the games. How to bet, how to play poker, blackjack, craps, we went over the lingo over and over again.

We started with Poker games, like Texas Hold em, Five Card and Seven Card Stud, Straight Poker, Five Card, and Seven Card Draw. They would walk me through and taught me what a good bet was and what was a dumb bet. They taught me how to gamble; then, they tried to teach me how to deal with the various games. Poker and Blackjack, I got. Craps, paying the odds, learning the lingo, and the protocol that was my problem area. They provided me with several books on gambling that I studied at night in my room, and they would quiz me the next day.

Towards the end of each training session, the agents would run an undercover scenario that would, at times, have me acting as a gambler and at other times as a dealer. They wanted to see if I looked comfortable playing the games and using the lingo. They would correct each mistake I made, and there were plenty and would applaud my triumphs - which were much fewer. They always let me determine how to act in each scenario then would correct what needed to be fixed. And they did that in a way to ensure I understood what they were saying and then they would test me again to make sure I didn't forget.

After each day of training, I was sent back to my room with my notes and books on gambling. I studied at night in my room, and the next day I would get tested on what I had learned the day before. I was used to nailing my tests as a new agent while at the FBI Academy. But it seemed no matter how many hours of studying I put in, and I didn't seem to play like a pro or even a close to an experienced gambler.

On day five, I was frustrated. It was evident that Cards and Craps were indeed not my forte. If I were a betting man,

I would have said the chance of me becoming a gambler was zero percent.

I had just spent three hours playing poker, getting my ass kicked. Pete had all my chips piled in front of him. If it were an actual game, I'd be leaving broke. The other agents I had played with had all left to get lunch. I sat at the table, studying the chips, the cards, and going over my mistakes.

"You okay, man?" Pete asked.

"Least it wasn't real money," I shrugged.

"Listen. No one can learn to play like a pro in a week. It is impossible. True gamblers have cards in their blood," Pete said, trying to reassure me.

I appreciated his efforts, but that wasn't making me feel any better. I had the opportunity of a lifetime in front of me, and the only thing holding me back was cards, dice, and jargon. Pete began scribbling on a piece of paper. When he was done, he handed me a cheat sheet on how to calculate payoffs on a craps table and what beats what in poker.

"Here. You are going to need this," Pete said, a half-smile forming across his wrinkled face. I was very appreciative of Pete's efforts and those of the other agents. Their efforts proved just what an FBI agent will do for his fellow agent. I will forever be grateful.

CHAPTER

13

There is an art to creating a persona. Every single detail needs to be thought out. Every question requires an answer just like real life. Going undercover is more than just fitting in. It is becoming someone new that is trying to start over in a new place. This new person (the undercover agent) is rarely from the location they are being placed. They rarely have a family, because setting up a family requires too many levels of lies, and too many things can go wrong. The agent is typically looking to buy some sort of contraband or attempting to get others to do something illegal. Hard to do when you don't have anyone to vouch for you. You need to find friends and fast.

Joe Pistone taught me to keep your undercover persona as close to your own as possible. If you stray too far from your true self, you will inevitably make a mistake. And that mistake will come back to haunt you possibly even get you killed.

The story of my undercover persona went like this:

I was from Louisville, Kentucky, with a minor criminal background focused on establishing and operating illegal gambling houses in the Louisville area. I was supposed to be a major money launderer for a local but very profitable drug organization that dealt mostly with marijuana. Marion County, Kentucky, which is located just outside of Louisville, was well known for its sinsemilla marijuana, a very potent and expensive form of a marijuana product that contained no seeds. I had no family and was looking to start a gambling operation in the Cleveland area. My challenge, I was a stranger that needed to convince a group of police officers to protect my gambling operation.

Just like Joe Pistone in *Donnie Brasco,* if you want to sell your story, you need to not only be confident in your background story, but you have to know your story inside and out. You need to lose yourself and become your story. If not, your investigation will go nowhere, and your targets will see right through it. It's not easy.

Now a name. The Bureau lets you pick your name. I decided on Brad Ray Morgan. I had always liked the name Brad for some reason. I thought it fit me better than Ray. But it turns out the key to a name is that you answer when it's called. The crew from Quantico and I ran through numerous scenarios, all of them included calling me by the name Brad. Each time they called out 'Brad,' I failed to respond or react.

This was a problem, so we decided after discussing this at length that I should just go with Ray. I kept Brad as my first name on my driver's license and all documentation that was created but was called Ray. It was a good thing I learned this before I started the undercover operation, or it would have gone nowhere. I can only imagine how ridiculous I would have looked by, not responding to the bad guys when they were calling me Brad. Just like I said, keep it as close to your true self as possible,

I had my story, knew my name, and now I had to establish my background. I had to be backstopped. Backstopping is the term used in law enforcement that refers to creating a history for the undercover agent and the operation. The FBI now has the premier backstopping unit in all of the law enforcement. This unit does everything to assist the undercover agent in preparing his background, from Social Security numbers to criminal records. Whatever the undercover agent needs, this unit provides it. Driver's License in your undercover name for a particular state. Boom, this unit gets it for you. Credit history in your undercover name. Done. Prior residence, bank account, car, apartment. I have even seen this department create a yearbook for a man who never existed. Whatever you need, they can get.

I was given the task of setting up proof of previous employment, residences, and arrest history. My first order of business set up a work history. For this, I went to Marcus Paxton, the owner of a local, family owned business in Louisville, Kentucky. I had worked with Marcus on a drug investigation that had involved his delivery trucker drivers. These drivers were making legitimate deliveries to Mr. Paxton's business, but before their trip, they would send FedEx packages to Mr. Paxton's place of business with their name on the box. The truck driver, after making his legitimate delivery, would then go to the office to pick up the Fed-Ex package with his name on it. All seemed on the up and up, except that the package contained 2 pounds of cocaine.

According to Marcus, this scheme had been going on for some time. It was not discovered until one of the packages accidentally tore open during transit. The mailroom clerk found a white powdery substance and notified Marcus, who in turn contacted the FBI Louisville Division.

I worked with Marcus for several weeks. Together, we set up a small sting. I told Marcus that the next time a package came in, that was addressed for a driver to contact me. I would go to the location, examine the package, bring a drug-sniffing dog, and his handler from the Louisville Police Department. If the dog "hit" on the box, we would set up an arrest team at the scene and wait for the driver to arrive. It took only three days for me to get a call from Marcus saying there was a package. I responded with the dog, and we had a hit. I put an undercover agent in the mailroom to wait for the driver to come and pick up his package.

When the driver arrived, he asked for his package. The undercover agent retrieved the package from the mailroom along with a document that required the driver's signature. The undercover agent asked the driver for identification to ensure the name on the package and the signature on the document matched. The undercover agent asked if the driver if this was indeed his package. The driver confirmed that it was, and the undercover agent handed over the package to the driver. This was recorded and was transmitted over our radios as well. The arrest team could hear exactly what had happened.

As the driver walked back to his vehicle, he was approached by the arrest team who had obtained a search warrant for the package, and once they confirmed that it was cocaine, the driver was arrested. We then offered the driver an opportunity to work with us to determine who the supplier was and where they were located. The driver begrudgingly agreed to cooperate and provided us with all of the important details of how this group operated. He also informed us that his supplier was located in San Francisco, California. Once we had all of the pertinent information, we forwarded that information to the San Francisco FBI, and they did the rest.

Mr. Paxton and I developed a friendship over those couple of weeks. Based on our trust and the friendship we developed, I asked him if he could help me establish a work history. I also requested that if anyone ever inquired about my employment to vouch for me. He was more than happy to do these things. A few months into my undercover operation, someone from the Cleveland Police Department called and asked about me working there. Marcus did his job well.

I then worked with the Louisville Police Department to establish an arrest record for myself. I wanted to provide proof that I had a past in the drug and gambling trade. A Lieutenant in the Louisville Police Department worked with me to put my fingerprints in the system and created an arrest record. They flagged my names and prints, noting if anyone inquired on my name to refer them to the Lieutenant.

Several months into my UCO, we received a call from an agent, an FBI agent in the Louisville Office, notifying us that there was an inquiry from the Cleveland Police Department and that the Lieutenant had handled it appropriately.

Lastly, to establish a residence history, I worked with a real estate agent who was married to an FBI agent.

With everything in place, I was ready to move to Cleveland to take on the most challenging task of my life. I was excited yet apprehensive. Everything I had done in my life before this, I had plenty of time to prepare. Not this time. I was flying blind. All I had was my Donnie Brasco book to rely on. This time there would be no excuses, no explanations. This was either going to be a success or a failure. I did not want to end up on 60 Minutes. Yet, somehow, I felt exhilarated.

CHAPTER

May 1989

I put the last suitcase into my 1987 Oldsmobile Cutlass Supreme; the sedan packed to the brim with all my belongings. I took one last trip back into the house. My two boys were standing at the door, tears trickling down their little faces.

"Please, daddy, don't go," Ross pleaded.

I picked him up in my arms and gave him the biggest hug. "I wish I didn't have to, but I do. And you guys and your mom will be in Cleveland soon enough. I am going to pick out a great house for us!" I said, trying to console him.

"Boys give daddy a hug. We will see him real soon," Lynn said, helping me out. She was very supportive, but I knew she was not happy.

Lynn and the boys had to remain behind in Louisville until my final orders were approved. That could take a few months, which would be much harder on Lynn than it would be on me. She was working full-time for Delta and still had to take care of two young boys.

I hugged Lynn tight. "I am going to miss you," I said, holding back my tears. She wiped them away from my eyes.

"We will be fine," she said, forcing a smile.

"I love you," I told her as I closed the door behind me.

I arrived in Cleveland five and a half hours after I departed my family home in Louisville. I pulled into the Hampton Inn near the airport around 1 pm. This was to be my first stop until I found an undercover apartment, and I only had two days to do this and sign a lease.

I checked into my hotel room, unloaded an overnight back, and set to the streets to find a building that I thought would work. I drove around for nearly two hours when I saw a sign outside a high-rise building in North Olmsted.

"This looks like as good of an option as any," I muttered to myself. I pulled into the parking lot and made my way to the leasing agent. In the next hour, I had signed a lease for a one-bedroom, one-bath apartment with a small kitchen and living room. The building had underground parking. I reserved two parking spaces in the apartment building's garage. I then hit a local Rent-A-Center and picked out a couch, a love seat, a queen-size bed, and a dresser. That was all I needed to furnish my apartment. They said they would deliver my goods in two days. I was on a roll!

Once I had my undercover apartment, I was able to open bank accounts in my undercover identity using my new undercover address. I opened a personal checking and savings account as well as a checking account for my new tee shirt shop, which was Brad Ray Morgan's 'day job.'

After the banks, I stopped by a local car dealership. I also had to lease an undercover vehicle, something that Brad Ray Morgan, pot dealer, and gambler would drive. I was used to driving a family or a bureau car. I had to pick out something that didn't say 'I'm a dad.' I walked the lot and found a 1987 Cadillac Deville that I leased for about $400.00 a month.

As the sunset over Lake Erie, the dawn of my new life was rising. I hit my bed hard. The next day would be more of the same. I had to find a location to rent for my new tee shirt shop and start my new business—all in a day.

I woke up early the next morning. I hit the streets and got in my six-mile run. I then stopped at the hotel gym and got a workout in. I then headed out to build a tee-shirt business—my first order of business, a location. I needed a storefront that could also house my underground gambling operation. Dan suggested I look at a location on Lorraine Avenue on the West Side of Cleveland.

Now, in case running a casino wasn't hard enough. I had to figure out how to run a tee-shirt print shop. A tee-shirt shop would not have been my choice of cover. Dan chose this. His informant told him that this would be the perfect 'in' to all of the bars and cops. So, a tee-shirt shop it was.

I scoured the west side of Cleveland and found the storefront Dan had suggested to me earlier. There were two storefronts side by side I rented both as Dan had suggested. One for the tee-shirt shop the other for the future casino. Having not had much experience in the tee-shirt business, I couldn't be sure, but I thought it would be a perfect location. Plus, both spaces were vacant, and I was able to take over the next day. This would allow the FBI Tech Agents, the wires and pliers guys as we referred to them, to get a jump on installing all of the surveillance and recording equipment. Dan would later rent an office space in the same building on the third floor. Our tech agents went inside and wired the place with monitors and recorders that were used to collect the evidence. Either Dan or Rick would be there in the third floor office space to operate the equipment whenever the casino was up and running.

It turns out the real estate was the easy part. I then had to purchase inventory, silk screening equipment, and everything else needed to run a legit working tee-shirt business. Through Dan's research, I was provided the name of a company that sold this kind of equipment. I contacted the company and purchased a silk screen printing press station, a heat press transfer machine, and all of the necessary accessories with the understanding that they would deliver the equipment to my tee-shirt shop within two days. I also purchased a large inventory of iron on printing decals. The silk-screening machine was mostly for show as I sent most if not all of the silk-screening work out to a company in New Jersey. I handled the heat press transfer and the iron-on decals in the house.

I was never to report to the FBI Office in Cleveland. Dan and Herb did not want me to be seen in the office as there were task force officers from the Cleveland Police Department working in the FBI office. They did not wish for me to be seen by them or anyone else in the office not assigned to the Corruption Squad. It was their understanding that no one could be trusted. Thus, there were only a few agents on the Corruption Squad who were ever made aware of my arrival and assignment. At this early stage of the investigation, Herb, Dan, and Rick were the only ones on the Corruption Squad who knew what I looked like. There was simply just too much at stake, and the risk of anyone knowing my face was too high. There were only a handful of FBI Cleveland employees who even knew I existed. This was a well-kept secret, and only those that needed to know would have that information.

On day four, after I arrived in Cleveland, we had our first team meeting. I rented out a small conference room at the Hampton Inn, where I was staying. I had a pot of coffee and donuts ready to greet my team.

The five team members I would be working with arrived at 8 am on the dot.

"Good-morning, Ray," Dan Estrem, my case agent, said as he walked through the door. Dan was about 5'11" with a head of thick black hair. He was the most energetic, confident, and determined agent I had ever met. He was Inspector Erskine, sans the fancy suits and ties, and he made me feel like I was in the middle of a television show. Dan poured himself a cup of coffee and sat down at the conference table. Dan was a whiz with the FBI rules, regulations and the insurmountable paperwork involved in undercover operations and all that goes with it (i.e., Court ordered Wire intercepts, the never-ending amount of reports that must be submitted to FBIHQ and the DOJ, etc.) Dan made sure never to let any of the bullshit and politics involved with FBIHQ, DOJ, and other agencies touch me.

My contact agent, Rick Hoke, took a seat next to Dan. Rick was a consummate professional in every sense of the word. Rick was my lifeline, and Dan kept the bullshit away from me. Rick was to keep me informed and up to date of what was happening within the FBI. As an undercover agent, you lose touch of who you are and what you do for a living. Rick was going to be the person who reminded me that I was not Brad Ray Morgan.

John Lavoie was my intended contact agent, but he received his office preference (OP) and left town. John was a great guy, but I was thrilled that Rick was on the job. Rick was often referred to as the Poster Boy for the FBI due to his clean-cut appearance and professionalism.

Herb Cohrs, who was the squad supervisor, and was one of the best leaders I ever worked for throughout my FBI career, grabbed a jelly donut before he took a seat on the other side of Dan. Herb was Dan's biggest supporter, and Herb made sure that Dan stayed up to date on all the reporting requirements and was often a good filter between the executive staff, FBIHQ, and Dan.

SAC Bill Branon took a seat at the head of the table. Mr. Branon was the head of the Cleveland FBI field office. He was one of the most impressive SACs I have ever known. He was impeccably dressed and possessed a booming voice. "You ready for this, Morrow?" he asked, leaning back in his chair.

"I think so, sir," I replied.

Assistant United States Attorney Bob Bulford was assigned to prosecute the case. I had typically never enjoyed working with attorneys, but it was a necessary evil. It was his job to ensure we were erring on the side of the law. Bob was one of the youngest Assistant United States Attorneys in office and was new to the Northern District of Ohio's United States Attorney's Office. He was aggressive, eager, and was willing to take calculated risks unusual for an AUSA. I was glad that he caught the case.

I was so privileged to be surrounded by such a fantastic team. I knew that these guys would have my back and that they knew what they were doing. They had to have seen something in me to give me this role. They were all too smart not to know what they were doing.

"Thank you all for being here for our first official team meeting on operation SHIRON," Dan said.

SHIRON? Was that our code name?

"SHIRON?" I questioned aloud. Hoping I did a decent job to hide my dislike of the name.

"SHI for Shirley and RON for Ron," Dan said.

There were so many great code names. Operation Sun Apple was the name of the case lead by Joe Pistone, aka Donnie Brasco. Operation Desert Glow was an investigation in Colorado against a company that made plutonium triggers for nuclear warheads. Operation Rap Crack was a case in Louisiana following a rap group dealing with cocaine. And my favorite of all Operation Greylord was an undercover investigation that targeted corruption in the Chicago, Cook County judicial system. The list of great code names goes on and on. And I got Operation SHIRON. I know you shouldn't judge a book by its title, but I would not have picked the name. But Dan was not someone who cared much about fancy window dressing; he focused on the tasks at hand. SHIRON could have had the code name "123," and Dan would have been okay with that. Dan just wanted to get the job done. As far as Dan was concerned, there was no time to come up with a fancy code name.

Boring code name aside, Dan was ready to pull off as

complex of an undercover operation as any with a fancy name. Possibly more complex. We were going after cops. Crooked cops. And truth be told, they knew how to run an undercover operation just as well as I did. They knew what they were looking for. They knew our tactics and tricks. We needed to be prepared, more prepared than going after your typical bad guy. Because these bad guys had badges and guns. We had to dot every 'I' and cross every 'T.'

We spent this first meeting, making sure every detail was covered. We discussed policies and procedures and the Attorney General Guidelines on Undercover Operations. We went over some of our subjects and suspect locations that Dan wanted me to become acquainted with. We talked about predicating each subject and the scope of the investigation. I was to stay within the parameters established within the Group I Proposal. Dan made sure that I had read the Group I proposal and that I understood it implicitly. We discussed how we were to contact each other. Dan discussed having surveillance cover me at night when I was going from bar to bar. We explained how I was to record all conversations and then draft FD 302s as soon as possible that would summarize the discussions and who was on the tapes. We also discussed how I would store the recordings until I could get them to Rick. I spent the next several days reviewing everything my team and I had gone over at our meeting.

My next task was to set up the tee-shirt shop. Dan provided me with an "employee" at the tee-shirt shop, an agent named Winnie Cooper. Winnie was to help me set up all of the equipment, display cabinets, shelves, inventory, and my office. Winnie was a great help and made the tee-shirt shop look presentable. I followed the instruction manual that came with the silk-screening press and practiced for several days until I had it down pat. I was all set to do small orders, but bulk orders would be outsourced.

Two weeks later, I moved into my new apartment in North Olmstead, Ohio. I couldn't believe it. I had set up a whole new life and business in just under two weeks. I felt that maybe, just maybe, I could pull this thing off.

CHAPTER

15

SHIRON – May 1989

Every undercover investigation is unique and different from the one before. Each one has a distinct personality, different crime, diverse demographic. There are unexpected and unanticipated events that occur throughout an undercover operation, and how they are addressed or avoided is unique. The biggest thing that sets each investigation apart is the turning point, the thing that transpired along the utterly unexpected way, even though we try to ensure that every move within an undercover operation is well choreographed.

SHIRON was set in motion over a year before Dan ever realized he was going to need an undercover agent. Almost as soon as Dan arrived in the Cleveland Division, he began to develop this investigation from the ground up by developing and utilizing informants and other sources. Dan also used some available sophisticated techniques, such as wiretaps.

Dan was the lead agent and did the majority of the street

work on his own. Dan did get help from other squad agents who he assigned to assist him on occasional surveillance, reviewing records or other tasks that Dan just did not have time to do himself once the investigation started to build. Dan had established relationships with sources and informants who trusted him and would not work with anyone else. With that being said, the case was all on Dan's shoulders; it was either going to be a success or failure based on Dan's efforts. His neck was on the line far more than mine.

Based on Dan's efforts, the Cleveland Division established a public corruption squad around Dan and the investigations he was generating with his informants, cooperating witnesses, and the investigations he was developing.

After I had settled in, I was ready to go. It was time to meet informants. These guys were going to be critical to the success of the operation.

Dan set up my first meeting with a guy named Benny. I was told to meet Benny at a coffee shop on Lorraine Avenue near my tee-shirt shop. Dan gave me a description of Benny and told me he was easy to pick out among the clientele in this particular coffee shop. Dan was right. Most of the people in the shop were businessmen and people who lived in the neighborhood. And then there was Benny. Benny was your typical biker, with long brown hair, and it was quite apparent that Benny liked motorcycles. He wore a leather vest with motorcycle emblems, riding boots, gloves, everything but a helmet. Even though he was involved in a motorcycle accident that left him somewhat disabled, he still refused to wear a helmet whenever he rode. Benny's minor stroke partially paralyzed the left side of his face, which adversely affected his speech. Benny slurred most of his words and drooled when he tried to speak quickly.

Per Dan's instructions, Benny was waiting for me. Dan had described me to Benny, and we were both able to pick each other out instantly. We shook hands, and I sat down and ordered us coffee when the waitress came by.

I had a hard time understanding Benny at first but got used to the way he spoke as time went on. Dan had been working Benny as an informant for several months. Benny was easy pickings because he was always getting himself into trouble with the law and would then offer to help law enforcement to help him get his charges reduced or dropped.

Dan was introduced to Benny by a fellow law enforcement officer who knew Dan was looking for informants with possible connections to public corruption. Benny, along with other informants Dan was working, provided information that identified corrupt police officers and the local bars where they hung out. This information focused on gambling, bookmaking, stolen property, and other illegal activities where police officers were involved. This information helped Dan initiate his undercover operation.

Benny was supposedly well connected with several Cleveland Police Officers that were involved in illegal gambling operations. Dan wanted Benny to introduce me to these police officers and suggested we do that at the local bars where these officers hung out.

My first meeting with Benny was like a game of cat and mouse. He didn't trust me, and I didn't care for him. We drank our coffee and discussed what Dan had laid out. We talked about the police officers and the bars we would be visiting - Walt's Café, The Romper Room, and others in the area. Benny spoke about some of the police officers he knew to be involved in bookmaking operations and illegal gambling operations and how he became aware of this information. Larry also mentioned a few local bars he knew that ran drug rings and ran stolen property.

"I know these bars like the back of my hand. I'm a regular," Benny insisted.

"And these guys trust you enough just to bring me into your circle?" I asked.

"I'm going to introduce you as a friend of my cousin from Kentucky," he said, sipping his coffee.

I was uneasy around Benny, and I wasn't sure why. I was not convinced that he could do what he stated he was going to do. I just didn't think cops would hang with this guy. But Dan had been working with Benny and was confident that Benny could do what he said. I figured that I just had to get comfortable with Benny and that it would probably take a little time.

We left the coffee shop and headed to the tee-shirt shop I set up as my cover. It was called Simply Tees. I hated the name, but that was what I was told it was. After we arrived at the tee-shirt shop, Benny informed me that he and Dan had an agreement that the name would be Simply Tees. Benny's wife liked the name and asked Dan if that was okay. Dan could have cared less about the name, so he agreed. So now, I am working in an undercover operation named SHIRON and own and operate a tee-shirt shop called Simply Tees. *Outstanding.*

Now, biker clad Benny was supposed to be my buddy. My pal. Thus, the undercover coordinator thought I should match his personality. They suggested I become a leather-clad cowboy. They sent me out to buy a leather vest and cowboy boots. I felt ridiculous. I wore them both once and never put them on again. It just was not me. I was very uncomfortable and very self-conscience. I knew if I was going to succeed, I had to be myself. After I whined and complained incessantly to Dan about not wanting to wear cowboy boots and leather vest Dan acquiesced. I worked Benny for several weeks. Benny made some introductions but never made the important ones that he had told Dan he would.

Benny first introduced me to Bill and George at Walt's Café. Bill and George worked for Bud Branson, a Cleveland Police Officer who ran a bookmaking operation out of his bar. Bill was a burly bearded older man who worked as a bartender. George ran the bookmaking operation from the bar for Bud. Bill loved to drink, which tended to make him a not so good bartender, and George had a terrible odor and a severe case of bad breath and was also a big drinker. I had to deal with him quite a bit, and it was hard to keep from throwing up. He smelled that bad. I could sense that Bill and George knew Benny but were not good friends and found him more of a pain than a comrade. As we sat at the bar at Walt's Café, Benny would try to engage Bill and George in conversation. Benny would talk and talk, and I could tell that Bill and George would do their best to get away from him.

I spent several weeks working Bill and George and barely acknowledged Bud. I placed bets on various sporting events with George on almost a daily basis. Bill and George asked me all kinds of questions. They wanted to know where I was from, and what brought me to Cleveland. They wanted to hear about my family. And with each answer I provided, they came up with more questions. They were covering all angles to see if they could poke holes in my story.

As time passed, Benny was continually instructed by Dan to introduce me to specific targets and to be at certain places when I was there so that the subjects could see me with Benny. The majority of these targets were police officers that Dan had information on that they may be involved in shakedowns and bookmaking operations and which bars these officers were known to socialize. Unfortunately, Benny was not showing up at the set locations, and consequently, I wasn't getting introduced as Dan had instructed. This went on for several weeks, and the operation was going nowhere with Benny. However, I was working on other angles at various bars, clubs, and other local businesses. I was getting to know the locals and was working out who may be interested in gambling and perhaps if they would be interested in my casino. I seemed to be accepted more readily by the subjects and their associates when Benny was not with me.

However, Benny was telling Dan quite a different story, boasting about his efforts and accomplishments in the case. Finally, I had to stop this. I went to Dan and explained to him what was going on. Dan requested that I give Benny one last chance. That night we planned a meeting at The Romper Room, a little dive bar on the west side of Cleveland. I took my place at the bar around 10:00 pm, a half-hour before we were scheduled to meet. I waited for over two hours for Benny, but he never showed up.

The next day I decided to end the charade. I asked Benny to come down to the T-shirt to discuss. Benny walked into the shop. He seemed annoyed that I had asked him to come in. "Why did you call me here?" he asked.

I took a few steps back to make sure that Benny was positioned directly in front of the cameras. Benny knew my office was wired, so I wasn't sure how honest he would be, but I figured I would try to get the truth.

"Why didn't you show up last night?" I asked.

"I did. I must have missed you," Benny shrugged.

"Benny, I was there a half-hour before we were supposed to meet and stayed for several hours."

Benny started to mumble and stumble on his words. So, I continued, "And I spoke to Dan this morning. You told him that I didn't want to be introduced to one of the subjects, and I wouldn't listen to you last night."

Benny became angry and irrational when presented with the truth. He stormed out of my shop. I called Dan to meet me so I could show him the tape. With that, Benny was off the operation. I truly believed if Benny stayed on much longer, he would have gotten me killed. I believed Benny was hesitant to get me involved as he saw he was losing his time with Dan as Dan was spending the majority of his time with me and this both bothered and scared Benny that he might lose his pay day.

I couldn't blame Dan, though. Many agents have a hard time believing their informants would lie to them, especially when they are paid for their information and cooperation.

I spent days working at the tee-shirt shop. I would leave periodically for sales calls to the local bars, restaurants, and other local businesses to see if I could sell them tee shirts, sweatshirts, hats, and other apparel with their business's name or logo. I also had a decent amount of sales from people who happened to be walking by the shop stop in. I averaged approximately 1 -2 orders. Not too shabby for a business that was a front for a sting.

I processed and did the silk-screening and iron on decal orders. The silk-screening orders came from the local bars as well as from other local businesses. The tee-shirt shop turned out to be an excellent way for me to introduce myself, as well as to ingratiate myself to some of the bars that Benny had previously identified for Dan.

My tee-shirt shop was on Loraine Avenue, a main thoroughfare in the West End of Cleveland. It was part of a city block of two to three-story buildings that were connected and lined the street. The buildings were old, and most of the storefronts were closed and empty. On the street behind our building were mostly older residences with tiny yards, if any. Most of the buildings that ran along the main street in the neighborhood were storefronts. It was an ideal location.

My office was located towards the back of the Tee-Shirt Shop. It was a small square office that looked out on to the floor of the shop and at the front entrance. Behind my desk was a set of built-in built in bookcases with the cameras and surveillance equipment hidden throughout my office and storefront.

Opposite of the bookcase, along the wall, was a love seat. On the other wall was a long cabinet. The video recorder was hidden in the drop ceiling. The microphones were hidden in different parts of the room.

The entrance to the store had two large windows on both

sides of the front door. There was a large L-shaped counter and shelves that housed most of my inventory of Tee-shirts. Towards the back of the store, on the right-hand side, was my silk-screening equipment and more inventory. I also had the decals that were used for the silk-screening displayed on the walls. A camera and microphones hid in the walls and ceiling where the merchandise and press equipment were located.

As I prepared myself for the operation, Dan was readying the Cleveland Division. Dan was most concerned with my safety and made that a priority. Dan put together a handful of agents who were assigned to surveil me from the time I started my day until I made it back to my undercover apartment that night. I didn't meet them face to face but was able to communicate with them via a transmitter.

I knew from personal experience that following someone around all day is incredibly dull. I am sure they were going nuts, watching my mundane movements, and listening to all my conversations. Dan kept this surveillance going for the first few months of the operation and planned to discontinue the tails as I got closer to the subjects and more comfortable in my role.

I became efficient at silk screening tee shirts, jackets, hats, baseball uniforms, etc. I also had the assistance of another agent who worked in the shop as one of my employees. The first was Winnie. Winnie was eventually replaced by Paul. Both FBI agents who had also become proficient in the tee-shirt business and were outstanding in filling their roles. When I was out making my rounds at the various locations we were targeting, they would run the shop for me. When I was there, they were great company.

● ● ●

After putting in a full day of work at Simply Tees, I would head to my apartment, workout, and eat dinner. From there, I headed out to the bars. I typically arrived around 8 pm, and my night of barhopping would go on until 1:00 or 2:00 am. I would often visit several bars throughout the night. I would only spend significant time in one place if I felt that the conversations were valuable and made it worth my time. But I had to remember to either leave or take a bathroom break every ninety minutes. I only had 90 minutes until I had to change the tape in the little Panasonic recorder that I was wearing. There were times I would sit quietly and observe the dynamics of the various people interacting, trying to understand the relationships and who I should focus my attention on.

The bars I went to were old and small in size dark, dingy, and almost always had loud jukeboxes playing. Walt's Café was cut from the same mold. It had a small kitchen and a television. The bar was L Shaped and was situated right in front by the door. There were some booths and tables around the outer edge of the room. Most parking was on the street, but there was also a small parking lot in the back.

These bars were dirty, and the clientele questionable. On one occasion, I walked in and saw one of the patrons peeing right at the bar. It was disgusting. I did not drink much, but if I did, I would order a bottle of beer but preferred a can soda. At the end of the night, I would head back to my undercover apartment, review the tape recordings and then draft a brief FD 302 summarizing what and who was on the tape. I would also mark on the FD 302 if the conversation were pertinent or non-pertinent. Doing this would help the agents who would later have to listen and transcribe the tapes for court.

The next morning, I would be back at the Tee shirt shop at 8:30 am. During the first few weeks, I was running the tee-shirt shop during the day, going to the bars, or meeting with subjects. At times, I would have covert meetings with Dan or Rick to hand over my tapes or to go over operational issues. I was always on the run. Constantly thinking about the case.

During the investigation, I made it a point to have a reason for every meeting I was recording. I would ask myself, what do I want to get out of this meeting? What do I want to accomplish from this conversation? It could be as insignificant as just letting the targets and their associates get to see me and get to know me. Or it could be as crucial as getting a police officer to describe on tape in great detail how he is going to protect my gambling operation. I always had a purpose, and I never lost sight of it.

CHAPTER

16

A few weeks into the operation, I realized that I had disconnected entirely and disassociated with my real life. Everyone I knew, everything I associated myself with, was no longer a part of my life. My family, the FBI, my social life were all gone. I missed Ross and Blake's baseball games, school activities helping with their homework, playing in the yard watching their favorite cartoon and movies even going to Sunday mass with my family. It was all gone, and I missed it.

I also stopped going to church, as part of this separation process. I chose not to go to mass during my undercover operation, as I believed this was all a part of hiding my true identity, and that was part of my true identity. I honestly did not want them to know anything about who I was. The second reason was I was lying every day all day. That would have been one heck of a confession.

Before Benny was removed from the case for being a liability, he introduced me to Gary, another of Dan's informants. Although Benny knew I was an undercover agent,

Gary did not. After Benny introduced Gary to me (at Dan's direction), Gary informed Dan that Benny had some guy from Kentucky who was into gambling and wanted to set up a casino in Cleveland. This was brilliant. Now, not even the informant knew about my cover.

I met Gary about three months into the operation as I was moving away from Benny and was starting to run with Gary. This made the break and disappointment from relieving Benny as an informant much easier for Dan.

Gary was a young street-smart kid about 23 years old. He had dark brown hair, green eyes, solid build, and a tragic gambling problem. Dan instructed Gary to get close to me and find out all he could about me. After Benny made the introduction, Dan told Benny to back off and let me deal with Gary. The biggest problem I had with Benny was that the people Benny did introduce me to did not trust me in the beginning because they did not like or trust Benny. This was making it difficult for me to get these people to accept me. I found this out after we had dumped Benny. I may not have had any experience in undercover, but I was pretty good reading and understanding people.

Neither Gary nor Benny knew that the other was working for Dan. Gary thought he was double-dealing Dan by running his own high stakes games while providing Dan with information on other gamblers. Dan knew exactly what Gary was doing. Dan provided Gary my Kentucky criminal background and told Gary that the FBI was very interested in me. Gary worked me hard for Dan, and that worked out well for me and the investigation.

Dan had other sources who were keeping him informed on Gary, but Dan and I needed Gary since he was very close to Shirley and Ron. Dan instructed Gary to help me establish a high stakes poker game and a small casino. Gary even recommended and brought gamblers to play at my poker game. Gary started the ball rolling, and he did whatever I asked him to do. He was an ideal informant. And I finally felt like things were beginning to role.

July 1989

It took a couple of months and the help of Gary, but I finally began working with the people I thought I needed. As Joe Pistone stated in Donnie Brasco, "you never start at the top." Identify those around your primary target. Who does he trust? Who does he work with? Go after them. The first bar that we identified as having a corrupt policeman was Walt's Café. Walt's Café was owned and operated by Bud Branson, a Sergeant with the Cleveland Police Department.

Benny had pointed Bud out to me early on in our excursions to the bar but never could formally introduce me. However, over the course of a few months, I was able to build a relationship with Bill and George. Once Benny was out of the picture, Bill and George set up a time for me to meet with Bud.

"Bud. Come here. I want you to meet someone," Bill said, waving Bud over.

Bud was 45 years old but was rough. He had a potbelly and a thinning hairline. He was a Cleveland police officer with nearly twenty years on the job, and the job must have been hard on him. Bud was a disheveled drunken mess that lived above the bar. Even so, he was cautious and wary of new people.

Bud had larceny in his blood and used the position of authority and trust for his gain and benefit. Bud was manipulative, dishonest, corrupt, and he freely used his shield as a license to steal and coerce. Bud had no issues with accepting bribes or shaking down individuals who wanted to avoid prosecution or those he tried to intimidate. He was known to use the authority bestowed upon him as an opportunity to reward himself and his friends.

Bud walked over to me. I stood up, my hand outstretched. "Ray," I tell him.

Bill tells Bud that I am a good guy and that I have been placing bets with George, who ran Bud's bookmaking operation from the bar. Bud and I started to talk. Bud asked a lot of questions, especially about how I knew Benny.

"I think Benny is a no good, I don't trust him," I said with a shrug. Right then, Bud's demeanor changes and he lets out a loud chuckle.

"Asshole," Bud declared. At that moment, I knew Bud, and I hit it off.

One of the things I needed to do was to gain Bud's trust. After a few weeks of working Bud hard, I wanted to see if Bud would buy stolen liquor and cigarettes from me. I suggested to Dan, who then sought approval from FBIHQ to allow us to purchase a large shipment of liquor from Jim Beam and large cigarette shipment from Kentucky as well to sell to Bud. FBIHQ approved Dan's request.

I started working Bill and George, telling them that I had a large shipment of liquor that was stolen and needed to get rid of it. A few days of back and forth on this, and Bud got involved. Now, I am getting excited something is about to break. During this time, I tell Bill and George that I am going to operate a large stakes poker game at my shop. A few days later, I drive up to Walt's Café with a rental truck loaded with Jim Beam and cigarettes. I walked inside and motioned to Bud that he should come around back. Bud walks outside with me, and I lead him over to the truck open the back, and I can see Bud smile from ear to ear.

We argued on the price, but we eventually agreed on a dollar amount, and Bud bought the liquor and the cigarettes. It was all recorded on audiotape. I didn't care what Bud paid for the load, but as Donnie Brasco taught me, don't make it so easy to make the deal, make them work for it. It looks better. I believe this was a big step in gaining Bud's trust. Bud knew I was hanging out at some of the other bars and made sure I did not sell any of this liquor or cigarettes to them. He wanted to make sure he was the only one in town getting my deals.

August 1989

It took me more than a month to gain Bud's trust and get the space next door to my tee-shirt shop ready for a poker game. I worked with Gary to recruit six to eight poker players for a Friday night game.

The space I had rented along with my tee-shirt shop sort of mimicked the layout of the tee-shirt shop. I blacked out the windows of the shop and set up a giant poker table. I also set up a table full of food and drinks. Most of the guys were expecting alcohol, and it probably would have helped to keep the money flowing, but Dan, Herb, the DOJ, and the FBI would not allow it. That was a smart move. I kept asking Bud, Bill, and George to come down to play some poker, but they kept avoiding the place.

It was the day of my first poker game. I had never been so nervous in my life. I thought I was going to throw up. This was the real test. The hardest thing I would have to do thus far. I had to not only operate a high stakes poker game, but I had to participate with these gamblers. That first night I lost big, and I lost my bankroll fast. The gamblers I was playing against were almost professionals. They could sense I knew nothing about poker even though my self-created background said I was a big-time gambler. But obviously not a very good one.

Most of these gamblers were sent to my game by Gary. Gary was a known player in the gambling arena in Cleveland, and at Dan's instructions, he was bringing some of the best poker players Cleveland had to offer. Unlike Benny, this informant was doing what he was paid to do. These guys were beating the pants off me.

I continued to run a high stakes poker night every Friday night. But I could not get any police to come. Just big-time poker players. Dan told me, word on the street was that my game was the best in town. Big-time poker players in Cleveland were begging to get in. I thought that's just great. I'm busting my ass trying to get some police officers to come to my game, and all I'm attracting are the big-time poker players in Cleveland.

Every week, I would try to convince Bud, Bill, and George to come down and play or just sit in for a while. Every Friday night the poker game went on, and I would lose, and there was no Bud, George or Bill insight, I was also going to other bars and getting close with police officers at places like the Romper Room. I was able to recruit some great poker players but no cops.

One Friday night, just as we were getting started for another night of poker, one of the regular Friday night poker players came up to me, "Word on the street is you are law enforcement maybe even FBI."

Everyone in the room grew quiet, waiting for me to respond. It was apparent to me this was something on everyone's mind, and this individual was selected to be the one who asked.

I looked at him, and without hesitation, I said, "You're right, I'm the FBI, and you are all under arrest, let's go."

No one said a word. *Oh no, it is all over, I am going to New York for sure.* Finally, one of the players started laughing, and everyone joined in. "Shut-up and deal," the man yelled.

Donnie Brasco saved me here. If not for that book, I would not have been prepared to respond to that. As an undercover agent, you have to be prepared for just about anything even more so when you are going up against police officers.

CHAPTER

17

September 1989

My days were so consumed that I barely noticed that three months had passed since I last spent time with my family. When I finally received my official transfer orders to Cleveland, my family was able to make their way north to me. Lynn came up to Cleveland and began looking for houses. She begged me to join her, or to at least look at the house she was going to purchase for our family, but I was never able to find the time. She found a home in Strongsville, Ohio. I never even saw the place before I signed the necessary paperwork for the mortgage.

Lynn and the boys moved to Cleveland several weeks later. Lynn enrolled the boys into Strongsville schools and began settling in. She was still working for Delta, and I could tell she was overwhelmed. But there wasn't much I could do to help. I only made it out to see her and the boys twice in the first month she had moved to Cleveland. And I wasn't there for long. I had to make it to all the bars before I could head home. I would arrive home around 2 am. Everyone was asleep. I slide in bed next to her. I didn't want to wake her as she had to be at work bright and early. The next morning, we would be able to catch up for a bit before the boys woke up. I would have breakfast with them and then had to get to the tee-shirt shop.

Lynn and I both hoped that I would make it home now and then to be with her and the boys. And honestly, that was my intention. But little did I know, my path was being paved with good intentions.

October 1989

The fifth month of the investigation was underway, and I was consumed. I could not think about anything else. I lived and breathed the case I was all in. This was needed for an agent to accomplish the mission. It is not necessarily healthy for a human being, and the FBI knew that. I was ordered to report to The FBI Academy for my psychological assessment. The assessment included a four-hour psychological exam, which was a series of psychological assessment tests that included the Minnesota Multiphasic Personality Inventory (MMPI), which is a psychological test that assesses personality traits and psychopathology. This was then followed up with an interview with the Behavioral Science Unit Psychologist.

This was the second time I had taken the test. The first was just before I was selected and approved for the undercover operation. That test set the baseline for all of the other tests I would take. I did well. No problems. I was good to go and be the best FBI undercover agent I could be.

I let Gary know that I was headed to Louisville to tend to some personal matters and would be back in a few days.

When I arrived back in Cleveland, Gary called me, "I have a new contact for you. Meet me at the Silver Fox Show Bar on Scranton Road."

I felt a jitter in my stomach. I knew the name of the bar and the contact. It was Shirley Connor. Finally, after almost five months of being undercover, I was introduced to the lady the case was named after. Shirley was at least 45, you could tell that in her younger days, she was probably pretty, but time had not been kind to her and now looked as though the booze and smoke had beaten her. She had long blonde hair and had an over-the-top personality.

Shirley was always scheming and rarely considered the feelings of others, except for those closest to her. This was obvious as I watched her interact with her dancers and the customers at her strip club/bar. Shirley was confident in her abilities and believed she could accomplish just about anything she set out to do.

Shirley readily made known her accomplishments. Shirley was always direct when dealing with others no matter who it was, and she expected the same direct approach to her from others. Shirley never hesitated to take risks.

"Shirley, I want you to meet my buddy, Ray," Gary said.

"Nice to meet ya', Ray," she said, extending her hand out.

"Nice to meet you, Shirley. Nice place you have here,"

I said, motioning to her club. I didn't find it nice. In fact, it was making me uncomfortable. I wasn't a fan of strip clubs. Everything about it bothered me.

"Thanks," she said. "Lots of nice girls. You like any of them?" she asked.

"Not here for that," Gary said.

Gary explained to Shirley that I was running a high stakes poker game and was looking for more players. Shirley was receptive and friendly but a little leery at first as she did not know me, but she trusted Gary.

"Let me think on it," Shirley said after hearing the plan. "I will call you later, Gary."

That was an excellent first step! The next day Shirley called Gary and told him that she would have players at my place the following Friday.

Slowly, I had to ingratiate myself to the people here. I had to get them to like me, trust me, take me in, so to speak. Even though I was hanging out at local bars, I rarely drank. I seldom drank liquor. I believed I needed to keep my wits about me and keep my senses sharp as I was afraid if I did drink a little too much I could say or do something that could ruin this investigation in a heartbeat. Besides, I just didn't drink much beer or alcohol at this point in my life.

Early in the investigation, I once raised this with one of my fellow undercover agents Vinny Wincelowicz. I mentioned to Vinny that I was concerned because I was not drinking very much at all when I went to these bars, and I was worried the people I was trying to get close to would not trust or believe me. I mean they had to be thinking, why does this guy, who no one knows, keep hanging out at this bar and yet he rarely drinks? I was sure that was what they were thinking. I know that's what I would be thinking.

"Are you buying them drinks while you are there?" Vinny asked.

"I am," I replied.

"Then don't worry about that because no one cares whether you are drinking or not," Vinny said with a laugh. "Nobody cares."

Vinny was right because no one cared whether I drank or not. As long as I would buy them drinks, they were fine with me. They enjoyed my company. We had great conversations and developed friendships. Friendships that would never exist in my real life and would end as soon as the operation was over.

Running all night, working at the shop during the day kept me busy. Still, I had to attend weekly meetings at my undercover apartment, with Dan, Rick Herb, and we were usually joined by the Assistant United States Attorney, Bob. We would go over everything that had happened that week. From whom ever I met with, to details of those conversations. We discussed tactics that would encourage the police officers to protect my casino or even show up at the poker games. Usually, the meetings were very engaging, and for me, they were refreshing to be able to talk to and with FBI agents' people who believed in some of the same things I did. I found these meetings to be necessary for my sanity. It was a time to interact with peers and not the bad guys.

During the operation, at the end of each day, I would worry about every conversation I had with the subjects. I would ask myself: "What did he mean when he said...?" "Did he believe me when I answered ...?, "What did I accomplish today?" "Did they believe me?" I continually questioned everything I said and did. I would review the tapes and wonder.

The investigation haunted me. By that, I mean, I could not stop thinking about it. I was obsessed with the investigation, and I had very little time for my family.

CHAPTER

18

November 1989

Each Group 1 undercover operation receives funding for six months. At the end of the six months, a review is conducted to determine if another six months of funding is warranted. Our budget for the first six-month period was over $300,000. If it is determined that another six months is warranted, a new proposal is submitted by the field office and then approved by FBIHQ and the DOJ. We were getting near the time to decide if we were going to re-up for another six months.

I was, at this point, extremely frustrated as I had made many inroads and built trust and confidence in many of our subjects. Still, not a single police officer was yet biting on my proposal to operate a casino. Nor were the police giving me any indication they would be interested in protecting my operation. So, after another long Friday night poker game in which I again lost about $500 (thank God it was all on video), I asked Dan to come down to the shop where we had just finished playing.

It was now Saturday morning at about 10:00 am, and I had been up for over 30 hours. Dan had been upstairs monitoring the game and operating the video recording equipment until the early morning hours and was also exhausted when he arrived at the shop.

"Dan, I have been at this for almost six months, and we have just re-upped for another six. I have given this everything I have. I have not taken a day off. I work sixteen to seventeen hours every day, and from Friday morning thru Saturday morning, I work straight thru. And I am not getting anywhere. I cannot get the police to do anything. I think you need to get someone who knows more about gambling and casinos. Someone that maybe they'll believe in. I think I need to drop out of this for the good of the case." You have put together a great case and I have taken it nowhere, I said, a lump in my throat.

Those words were the hardest thing I ever had to say. I was giving up. That's not me. I learned early on life to never give up. My father instilled that in me from a very young age. Never quit, my father, used to say, often reciting a quote, *"there is no failure except in no longer trying."* But I believed that Dan had worked so hard getting us to where we were at this point. Maybe he could get someone to come in and take this home. At this point, I was exhausted and extremely frustrated.

Dan looked shocked and said to me, "you have done more and accomplished more than any of us had ever imagined. You have gained the trust of police officers, that quite frankly, we did not even think they would speak to you. The

SAC, Herb, and FBIHQ are all overwhelmed with what you have accomplished so far."

I was utterly shocked. I had thought I had failed miserably.

"If you want to quit, then there is not much, I can say. But if you do, I am shutting down the operation, because I will not be able to replace you with someone else, nor could anyone replicate what you have already done. And in all honesty, I did not think we would get past the first six months we just did not have much to go on. We did not have the predication even to approach the police, and now due to your efforts, we have the prediction," Dan continued.

We had managed to avoid any entrapment issues by showing that the police officer is predisposed to commit such an act. We had to prove that the officer has done this act before. We needed a record of the act.

"Now, because of your efforts, we have predication on several police officers, and they can't claim they were entrapped. And because you are so focused on the operation and your day to day interactions with the subjects, you didn't even realize how much you have accomplished," Dan finished. Boy, I needed to hear that. Dan was right. I had no idea what I had accomplished to this point, as I was just focused on what was happening right now. I needed to go back and review some of the recorded conversations and the trust I had built with these corrupt police officers.

Dan's words had energized and invigorated me more than ever to get this rolling. Although I was exhausted, exasperated, dejected, disappointed, I did not want to quit and end this operation because I knew full well; there were dirty cops in Cleveland. And more importantly, I owed Dan for having enough trust and confidence in me to select me as the undercover agent for his case.

Little did I know that prior to this, Dan had been fighting the front office as they were thinking along the same line as I was. They saw little apparent progress and also thought that perhaps they need someone else to take over the operation. But as he did with me, Dan eschewed their thinking and explained that he knew this was going to take some time, and just as he had informed me, he told them that I was making strides and was further along than he had anticipated I would be. Dan even played some of my record conversations with some of the corrupt police officers for them and they came around to Dan's way of thinking.

Dan explained to them that the information coming from the Title III intercepts was very positive. Dan reminded the front office that a police officer was not going to walk in and ask Ray for a kickback or bribe payment without the time and effort. That simply was not going to happen. Dan said it's going to take time and we are almost there. Dan had everyone's buy in at that point.

Dan was insulating me from all the bureaucratic bull crap, and I cannot express how important that is to the undercover agent as we have enough to worry about and do each day. Garbage like that would only make it more difficult for the undercover agent. All us undercover agents believe we are carrying the weight of the investigation on our shoulders. Heaven help those who think otherwise. Deep down, we, the undercover agent, know that is just not true. But we do have one hell of a lot on our shoulders.

I had very little time with my family over the past four months. If I did get some time, I had to first go to my undercover apartment until late at night and then go to the underground parking garage and get my second car, not my undercover vehicle and drive home. And I could never drive directly home I would backtrack and do all kinds of maneuvers to ensure no one was following me. That was as much for the protection of my family as it was the operation.

Usually, when I got home, it was late, and I would just go to bed. I would get up in the morning and have an hour with Ross and Blake before I would see them off to school. Lynn and I were growing distant because even when I was at home, I was continually thinking about the case. An undercover investigation engulfs a good undercover agent. It consumed all my thoughts and feelings. I steadfastly believe it has to, or you are just not doing it right. Or you are in it for all the wrong reasons.

Some undercover agents are in it for the thrill, or to get away from a bad relationship. Some undercover agents are only interested in working undercover for the cars, the money, expensive dinners, shows whatever excites them. The undercover operation never consumes them; they consume the operation.

I know, during that time, my time with my family seemed trivial and one dimensional to me. I was so focused on the undercover operation I simply could not focus on them. Lynn was doing her best to make our time together matter, but I didn't. The undercover operation controlled my thoughts and feelings.

Shortly after my family arrived in Cleveland, the boys settled into their new school at Kisner Elementary. A few days after they started school, Rick Hoke and Herb Kohrs, went to the school to brief the principal and teachers on my situation. They ensured Lynn and me that the school would not allow my children to leave with anyone other than Lynn or another FBI agent. They were asked to protect them and provide extra security. Periodically, my contact agent Rick and Herb would check in on my sons at their school. They could not define the issue at hand but made it clear that no one was to approach either of my sons.

There were several times Lynn wanted me to come home to spend some time with my boys, but she could sense I was not there emotionally, even if I did show up.

"Can you please do something with us? Anything?" Lynn begged me.

"Like what?" I asked, annoyed for no reason.

"I don't care. Even a trip to the grocery store will suffice," she begged.

"I can't. It's too risky," I told her.

"I am happy to go an hour away to shop. I just want to do something as a family other than watch you sleep," she replied.

She wasn't unreasonable. So, I gave in. We drove to a Giant Eagle grocery store in Youngstown, Ohio. It was over an hour away from my home base. I knew we were far enough away from home, and I would most likely not run into anyone I knew, but just in case I gave Lynn the protocol. I told her that if I saw anyone, I knew I would immediately walk away from her and the kids without a word. I did not want them following me or talking to me. I told her that I would walk down the street to a donut shop I had spotted, and she could come to pick me up there. I told her to go ahead and finish her shopping and act like nothing was wrong.

"That is silly, Ray," she said.

"It is not. And that is the way it has to happen. But I doubt that it will."

We get to the store. The boys are enjoying our family outing. And even as minor as it was, they were just happy to see me. I was picking up a box of Oreos when out of the corner of my eye, I see one of the bartenders from the Romper Room.

I immediately drop the box and take off out of the store. It was a good thing we had a plan in place. Lynn finished her shopping, and 30 minutes later, she picked me up at the donut shop I had picked out earlier. She was not happy, to say the least. And that was the last outing we had.

We continued another few weeks running the poker night, and I continued working my subjects. And then it happened. Bud, entirely out of the blue, came down to my tee-shirt shop for a visit. I had just seen Bud the night before at his bar, and we talked for quite some time never did he mention that he was going to stop by the tee-shirt shop to look over my operation. Bud walked in and stated that he wanted to see where I would operate my casino. I was ecstatic, but I could not let Bud see that. Finally! Finally, real progress! A sense of relief rushed through my body. I fought hard to contain my excitement. I could not let Bud sense what I was feeling, or he might just walk away. Bud made sure this visit was a complete surprise to me and I had to respond appropriately.

I took Bud around the tee-shirt shop and then explained that the casino would be operating out of the adjoining storefront. I captured all of this on video and audio. I had to walk Bud outside, and we entered through the front door. All the windows in that part of the building had been boarded up. It was pitch black, I turned on the lights and Bud could see the place was empty, except for the poker table I had been using for our Friday night poker games, but I explained to Bud where I thought the various tables and slot machines would go. Bud looked around and nodded asked again about what kind of games I planned on running. I told him I had one craps table, one poker table, one blackjack table, and some slot machines. Bud wanted to know when the casino would be operational. I told him Friday nights starting around 9:00 pm, and we would go until sometime Saturday morning. Unfortunately, we captured none of this conversation, but we then walked back over to the tee-shirt shop.

Once inside the tee-shirt shop, I went over everything we had just discussed next door with Bud again just to make sure that we got this on video. Bud asked about parking, and I told him there was plenty of parking both on the street in front of the shop on Lorraine Avenue, and in the back, there was a small parking lot as well as additional street parking. I said parking would not be a problem. Bud looked it all over and calmly informed me how many guys he thought he would need to protect the place and unbeknownst to Bud. It was all recorded. Bud said he would think about it and get back to me.

Bud left, and I immediately called Dan and asked him

to meet me at my apartment. I suggested that he bring Herb Rick and Bob as well. When everyone arrived at my apartment, I put the tape in, and we all watched as Bud and I discussed the casino. Even though Bud had not yet committed to providing protection, however, this was a huge step forward. There was a huge sigh of relief and euphoria from everyone. The celebration did not last long as Dan and Bob started to provide instructions on what we needed to do next.

CHAPTER

SHIRON the second six months

December 1989

A few days later, I heard from Bud. He asked me to stop by Walt's Café around 6 pm. When I got to Bud's, he was sitting at the bar. He waved me over to the seat next to him. I pulled out the ragged bar stool and slid in next to him.

"How's it going?" Bud asked, offering me a beer.

"Good. Friday night poker games are going well. Have some big fish each week. Still working on getting the casino up and going."

"That's why I called you here."

I nodded. *This may be the big moment!*

"I am willing to protect your gambling operation."

"That is fantastic," I said, trying not to seem too excited. This was a big decision for Bud. By agreeing to protect my operation, Bud was putting his complete trust and confidence in me, someone he did not know, someone who just all of a sudden appeared into his life. He was now willing to put his career, his life as he knew it, on the line. Bud wanted to let me know he would be in charge if he were going to hang his ass out to dry; he was going to do it his way.

Bud controlled the conversation I just listened intently I did not want to interrupt this fantastic evidence that was being recorded. If I said anything, it was an occasional okay or got it. Bud broke every rule when it came to protecting yourself and keeping yourself out of trouble. This moment was the moment that put our investigation on course.

Bud informed me that he would handpick the officers that he wanted on this job. He explained that he and his team would not just be providing security on the nights we ran the casino. He explained they would be working throughout the week to gather any intelligence to determine if the Cleveland Police Department was looking at our casino. He went on to instruct that if any type of intelligence was received that he would inform me, and we could not operate the casino that night. However, I still had to pay Bud, and his officers the agreed upon amounts, game, or no game. That was the price for his service and security.

Bud reiterated several times that he was in complete control. He would have it no other way. I had little to no say on how things would happen. He was the expert, and I was paying for his and his colleagues' expertise. He explained that payment was nonnegotiable and that I would have to pay the officers in the manner he prescribed, and in the amounts he recommended. First, Bud wanted $500 for himself and $250 for his officers to be paid at the end of the night. Second, I had to pay him, and he would pay the officers. I was not to pay the officers directly. Bud identified the first group of officers and provided a little background on each. Bud spoke about each officer, where they were assigned, how long they had been with the Cleveland PD, and told me of when and where they had done this type of work before (which was excellent for the predication we would need).

"What games will you have at your casino? Bud asked.

"Craps, blackjack, slot machines, and poker."

Bud nodded in approval, "Do we have a deal?"

"Yes, we do," I said, trying to hide my excitement.

I floated out of Walt's Café. Everything was finally falling into place. I could not wait to tell Dan and the gang and to play the tape for them. The next morning, I met Dan, Rick, Herb, and Bob at my undercover apartment and played the tape.

"That is wonderful, Ray," Dan said, excitement lining his voice.

"Great work!" Bob chimed in. You could just sense a huge sigh of relief in the room. We were all thrilled with the day's events, but we all knew deep down inside. This was just the beginning of a very long and winding road.

All the hard work, commitment, and patience had paid off, at least for now. I could not hold the excitement inside. I did it. Now, I just needed to get a craps table, one poker table, one blackjack table, and some slot machines. The slot machines were easy. The tables were a problem. We initially thought we could get them from FBI Quantico, but there weren't any available.

But I had a backup. During my first six months of the

operation, I had made numerous contacts. Cleveland FBI agents that were working drugs and stolen property cases had asked for my assistance. They had asked me to infiltrate one of the top fences for stolen property in Cleveland. I did. The culprit was a guy named Tony Malone. Tony was an older Italian guy who had his hands in everything if it were stolen in Cleveland; he had something to do with it.

I met Tony through another case agent's informant. I worked Tony using my undercover background story. Eventually, Tony took a liking to me. He even took me home for lunch one day. He had his wife cook an Italian feast. It was fantastic. After lunch Tony took to me his basement, which was filled with stolen property. He then took me to his warehouse, where he kept all of the big stuff. He tried to sell me some stuff right then and there. But I declined. Again, a lesson from Donnie Brasco, cops are always willing to buy something, anything, they always say yes. Donnie Brasco said to turn them down, and then they will never think you are a cop or law enforcement of any kind. You can always come back later, and they will never think twice because they trust you now.

During that visit to Tony's, I saw that he was building a craps table for someone. Now here I was, in need of a couple of tables. I went back to Tony and informed him of what I wanted to do, but I needed some tables.

"I will build you good tables," Tony said, with his thick Italian accent.

"I need the tables real soon," I told him, hoping he had something already available.

"I will build you nice tables and will have them delivered to you within two weeks."

"How much?" I asked.

"$1,500 for a craps table and $750 for a blackjack table."

"That is a lot of money," I tell him.

"They will be beautiful and delivered within two weeks. It is worth it."

Hopefully, he was right. When they were done, I paid him. And he was right. They looked great. Thing were finally rolling!

I was rushing around to get the casino ready, and things were finally rolling quickly. I was running on high gear and loving it. I was days from opening the casino when I got a request from Special Agent Herm Groman (one of the undercover agents at Quantico who had helped teach me the fine art of gambling). Herm happened to be the case agent on another police corruption case in Detroit, and he wanted me to pose as a money courier for a large-scale drug dealer. They needed me to be in Detroit for a few days. The day before I had to head to Detroit, Bud stopped by.

"You still on schedule to start this casino in a week?" he asked.

"I am. The tables arrived yesterday. They are beautiful," I told Bud.

"Nice. My guys and I are ready to go. Should I have them come by tomorrow to meet you?"

"Tomorrow doesn't work for me. I have to head to Kentucky for a few days." Bud and all my new associates thought that I still had business in Kentucky as a broker for large marijuana deals. I also let them know that I had a girlfriend in Kentucky who was a flight attendant. The covers worked, and little questions were asked.

That is until Bud decided to probe further on my girlfriend. "When do we get to meet this little lady friend of yours?" he asked.

"She flies a lot."

"I'd like to meet her," he replied.

I knew he was trying to follow my stories. It wasn't too surprising. I told him that when I came back, I would have her come into town.

"That would be good." Bud turned to leave, "See you next week, partner."

I flew up to Detroit met with Herm, the Assistant AUSA handling his case, and a few other undercover agents Herm had recruited for his undercover scenario. We all did our thing. My job was to fly into Detroit from Miami with a suitcase filled with what the cops, who would be protecting me and escorting me to a predetermined bank, believed to be cash. Once at the bank, I would meet another undercover agent posing as a bank executive who would take me into an office, take my suitcase, and provide me with paperwork, all while the police officers waited outside the bank. With my paperwork in hand, I walked outside and met the officers who promptly escorted me back to the airport, where I was to catch my flight back to Miami. Other undercover agents that were brought in worked on another part of the case that did not involve me.

Everything went as planned, and I came back two days later with my undercover girlfriend.

I called Bud to tell him I was home and asked him if he wanted me and my girlfriend to meet him at Walt's Café for a drink. He jumped on the opportunity. The more you know about a person's life, the more you can trust them. Dan had flown in an undercover agent, by the name of Kathy Stearman. She was one of the best undercover agents I had ever known.

Kathy was in her early thirties, had long brown hair, brown eyes, excellent physical shape, very attractive, but more importantly, very astute and exceptionally confident in her abilities. But I firmly believe Kathy's greatest attributes were her ability to listen and communicate. Kathy also just happened to be from Kentucky which really helped. She was a great sounding board for me when I needed to speak with someone who could cut through the bullshit and politics of the investigation. Kathy made significant inroads for me in this investigation every time she appeared. If I ever were the case agent on a Group I undercover operation Kathy would have been my undercover agent. She was that good.

When Kathy got up to use the restroom at the bar, Bud whispered to me, "Nice catch, man."

I could tell he was pleased that I had let him into my life. So, he could feel like he had something to hold me on as our casino was only days away.

CHAPTER

20

January 1990

Three weeks after my initial meeting with Bud, I had an entire casino set up. I had all the tables and the slot machines I needed. I had a back room set up for food and drinks. No alcohol was to be served per FBIHQ and DOJ. And most importantly, I had the police. Bud assured me that my casino would be the safest in town.

Now all I needed was some gamblers and some dealers. This was it. SHIRON, after all the months of hard work, after overcoming all the obstacles, was ready to roll. As in roll the dice. I was fired up for the operation, and it showed as I spent even less time with my family, and this was starting to become an even bigger problem. A problem that I just did not see coming, but Lynn sure did.

While we were getting ready to operate the casino, my

partnership with Bud began to grow. During football season, Walt's Café had a $5.00 all you can eat buffet on Sundays to support the Cleveland Browns. The buffet consisted of scrambled eggs, bacon, sausage, and hash browns.

I thought of an idea one night that would bring Bud and me even closer. I offered to make Cleveland Browns tee-shirts for the games. The tee-shirt would be brown, of course, with their logo on the shirt and a negative comment regarding their opponent that week. Buffet and the tee-shirt it would cost $10.00. The Tee-shirts were a hit. And now I am spending my Fridays, Saturdays and Sundays with Bud and his crew.

Every Sunday during football season, I would take the printed tee-shirts down to Bud's at 10:00 am. I would spend the day eating and watching and talking about Cleveland Browns football. That's when I knew I was good at this undercover stuff. If I could get people to believe that I, a devoted Pittsburgh Steelers fan, liked the Cleveland Browns, I had to be as good as Joe Pistone.

February 1990

It was a Thursday night. I was leaving Walt's Café around midnight, as I typically did on Thursday's and headed to my undercover apartment. Out of nowhere, I was hit with severe pains in my stomach. At first, I thought I might be getting the stomach flu and just needed to get back to the apartment quickly. But then another pain came, a pain so bad I had to pull over. I got out of the car to get some fresh air and started to vomit blood. I immediately thought of my father coming out of the bathroom with blood spattered all over. This is serious, I thought to myself.

I knew I had to go to the hospital. I could not contact Lynn for the sake of the operation, and I figured she wouldn't answer my call anyway. I pulled over at the first pay phone and called Dan.

"Dan, I need help," I said, my stomach in knots.

"What's wrong?" Dan asked.

"I think I need to go to the hospital now."

Dan was hesitant to meet there as one of the nurses at the hospital was Bud's sister. "Go to the ER. Check yourself in and call me as soon as you know something," Dan suggested.

I went to the hospital they ran some tests told me I had an ulcer and gave me a prescription. Luckily, I had health insurance in my undercover name, so I was able to check-in and got taken care of without any issue. Several hours later, I called Dan.

"I will be outside the ER entrance in a half-hour to pick you up," he said.

"I can grab a cab," I replied.

"Nonsense. Be outside at 3 am."

I got home around 4 am and was back at work the next morning.

I was now almost entirely absent from my family and real life. When I did make it home, the problems Lynn was facing daily were brought to my attention almost immediately. Lynn was working full-time at Delta Airlines, raising the boys on her own, and she made sure to remind me of that as much as possible.

When my family first arrived in Cleveland, I was excited to have a chance to see them. But now, the investigation was my life. The suspect my family. And as the complaints of my absence grew, my excitement disappeared. I spent the little time I had at home fighting with Lynn. And it annoyed me. I had much more pressing matters and problems to address in the operation, and unfortunately, that took precedent over any of the issues at home. I wasn't sure how much longer Lynn was going to take it, and even worse, I wasn't sure how much I cared.

I didn't have long to recover from my ulcer or to think about my family because we were now faced with the first significant issue to pop up in the investigation regarding the casino. We thought we would easily be able to record all the games and suspects, but our plan didn't work with Ohio's consensual monitoring law. The law made it so we could not just go with the Title III and record any conversations. We had to have at least one-party present who had agreed to be monitored. We needed a workaround. Dan came up with an incredible idea. We would have at least six undercover agents who posed as gamblers each night we ran the casino.

This allowed us to have FBI agents within earshot of almost all conversations, which, in turn, allowed us to over-come this obstacle. We always made sure that the undercover agents were assigned to various areas of the casino. We also ensured that at least one FBI agent covered all conversations with police officers. This eliminated entrapment and illegal overhears. This also satisfied our AUSA.

We then ran into another operational issue. FBIHQ and the US Attorney's Office would not allow us to serve alcohol at the casino. Typically, drinks were common and expected. I needed to find a reason that Bud would find acceptable. I told Bud that we couldn't have alcohol to avoid the risk of someone drunk driving and being pulled over and ratting us out. I told Bud that if that happened that he would probably be in more trouble than me. He agreed. That made it easy! We had enough problems to deal with already.

You could cut the tension in the air the first night at the casino. And it wasn't just me. The gamblers were unsure of the place at first, but as the night went on, they became more comfortable. The police officers appeared not to have a care in the world and that what we were doing was perfectly fine with them. I was nervous in that I wanted everything to go right. No hiccups or miscues. I had a craps, table, poker, and blackjack table. The craps table was jam-packed, and the blackjack table had a steady crowd. This first night I was working the craps table along with Herm Groman, Ed Keller, and a few other undercover agents. It went okay, but we all agreed at the end of the night that I needed to get some real craps dealers, a box man and stick man. There was also plenty of food that set up in the backroom that the gamblers thoroughly enjoyed it. We had a friendly crowd for the first night, and at the end of the night, around 9 am on

Saturday, I called Bud back to the backroom to pay him in front of the cameras. I started to count the money.

"Stop that shit. Just give me the money," Bud said.

I wasn't sure if he knew that when there is a possibility of a prosecution, the attorneys always want to have the money counted on camera or if he was just tired and in a hurry.

"Okay, fine. Send the other guys back one by one, and I'll pay them," I said.

"No, you pay me, and I will pay them."

I started to count the money, and he again instructed me to stop, "No, stop counting. Just pay me if you're short, I'll come back for the rest."

It had been a long day and night. I was too tired to argue and did not think it would matter. We had videotaped all the police officers who were there and recorded many of their conversations. And we were recording this conversation with Bud.

The next couple of weeks went the same as the first. Everyone was happy. The police were satisfied with their payments. The gamblers were delighted as they had a great casino to play. The FBI was happy as we were collecting evidence regarding Cleveland Police Officers being paid to protect an illegal gambling operation. I was relieved that the operation was going so well. The only person who wasn't happy was our AUSA Bob, who happened to be prosecuting the case.

I guess it's not fair to say he wasn't pleased, but he certainly wasn't satisfied. So, after a night of gambling, I was called to a meeting at my undercover apartment. Bob called the meeting. Dan, Rick, Herb, and SAC Bill Brannon were there.

"You are doing a great job, Ray," SAC Brannon told me. "After reviewing tapes, I must say how impressed I am that you have managed to maintain a relatively clean vocabulary amid all the foul language. That will go a long way with the jurors."

"Thank you, sir." Although it wasn't as if I was trying to keep it clean, it was how I typically spoke. Anything else would have been uncomfortable and unnatural.

"However, we do have one problem. The AUSA does not like that the only person you are paying is Bud."

Bob nodded in agreement.

"When I pay Bud for the officers, I always mention all the officers' names, and you can see and hear the police officers on the videotape. I also made a point to bring the officers into my office, in front of the cameras, to discuss the operation. And I always ask them if they are getting paid by Bud."

"It doesn't work. I need you to pay the officers individually, and I need you to count the money," Bob said, firmly.

These were two things Bud said could not happen. After much debate, Bob left, and I let my frustrations out on Dan and Rick.

"I hate attorneys," I said. I was agitated. No, I was pissed off.

No one can know what it is like to work undercover unless you've done it. No one can understand what is going through your mind and your subjects' minds. No one knows all that you have done to get to a point where the subjects trust you enough to commit an illegal act. No one knows the bullshit an undercover agent has to undertake. I knew that no matter how much I bitched, there was nothing we could do. Bob would be prosecuting the case, and these were their rules. They knew what they would need to convict these police officers.

The next Friday, just before we started the games, I called Bud into my office and discussed with him my intentions to personally pay the police officers at the end of the night. I told him that I was uncomfortable only paying him and not knowing if they are all getting their equal share. I reminded Bud that I had met individually with all the police officers and told them what they were going to be paid.

"I am worried you may not be paying them the agreed amounts and that may piss them off to the point that they may try and rob this place as they are all well aware of the amount of money that is here at any one time," I said, trying to come up with a way to get this done.

"Fuck you," Bud spat. He was very upset. "Ain't a chance in hell that will happen."

What do I do?

"Then this will be your last night as I know many other police officers who would like to fill your shoes," I replied.

Bud finally relented, "Fine. But I'm going to be in the room when you pay them."

Bud, you are outstanding. I will now have you not only accepting your payment but standing nearby, watching the others get paid!

Now, how was I going to count the money? I decided that I would no longer be prepared to pay them as I had paid

Bud in the past. When I had previously paid Bud, I had the money already counted in small stacks. Tonight, I was going to have the money all over the place. At the end of the night, I brought Bud into my office. I started to pull money in different amounts from my pockets and desk drawers. I handed it to Bud as I pulled the money from my various pockets and drawers and said, "Here Bud count that," And, he did, right on camera.

I would hand him some more money from the various locations and say how much is that? And Bud would count it, "That's fifty."

"Fifty?" I asked, to ensure it was captured on the recording. I then handed him some more, and he would do the same until we reached the agreed-upon $500 to Bud and $250 to each cop on duty. Then we would both say the final amount together on camera just as Bob had requested. I did the same with all the officers that worked that night. We all counted together. It was beautiful.

I could not wait for the next meeting with the AUSAs. I was able to show I was paying the other officers, and it was counted as well just as they had asked. My excitement quickly diminished when at the beginning of our meeting, Bob said he had another request, this one from the United States Attorney for the Northern District of Ohio.

They wanted me to get Bud to state that they are protecting the casino from any possible police actions. I protested this request vehemently to no avail. "How the hell do you want me to pull this off?" I asked angrily.

"That is up to you to figure out," Bob replied.

I had no idea how I was going to pull this off. Bud had already said back before we started that he was protecting the operation. Why would he need to say it again? Any idiot could see I was setting them up by asking them to make such a statement.

I was livid. I was busting my ass, and the AUSAs keep coming up with these ridiculous requests. The next Friday night following the latest AUSAs request, we were getting killed on the craps table. And the one killing us was an FBI undercover agent by the name of Ed Keller. Ed happened to be one of the agents that had helped teach me how to gamble at Quantico. At one point during the evening, I looked at the table and saw we had more chips out than I could pay. In other words, if at that point, the players wanted to cash in their chips, I would not be able to pay the entire amount. My stomach started turning; I needed to do something fast.

Ed spent a lot of time at the tables honing his craft. He was cleaning up at my tables. Around 1:00 am, I checked his table. He and others at the table still had more chips out than I could pay. What a night, on top of getting killed at the craps table, I kept thinking to myself, how the hell am I going to get Bud to inform me *again* that he and his crew are not only protecting the game but also gathering intelligence throughout the week? How am I going to do it without raising Bud's suspicions? And now, how the hell am I going to pay off all these gamblers if we keep losing? I could tell just by looking at the chips that were on the table, that I did not have enough money on hand to cash everyone out.

I motioned to Ed and some of the other undercover agents to individually meet me down in the basement. I needed them to give me their chips. I called Dan, who was watching via the monitor and asked, "Do you see what's going on?"

"Yes. I already called Herb and told him to go to the office and get some money from the safe. I will get it soon, and I'll call you, and we can meet."

It took a while, and it was now becoming morning, and the losses kept growing. Throughout the night, I kept meeting with the undercover agents and covertly taking back their chips. I finally met with Dan and got an additional $5,000.00. At the end of the night, we had lost approximately $26,000.00. I had enough to pay everyone to include the police.

But I had a better idea; I decided to tell Bud that I lost too much money and could not pay him or his guys. What could he say? He saw what happened and was unaware that I had gotten the chips back from the undercover agents or that I had received some additional funding from Dan. I hoped that he would scream and yell about how he and his guys protect the casino and ensure no one is looking at us or is onto what we are doing because of his work throughout the week.

I called Bud in and said, "Bud, I can't pay you tonight. I lost my ass." I waited for his response so that we could capture it on video, and I would have responded to the request of Bob.

"Okay, I understand."

That was it. I was devastated. I was hoping Bud would come to his senses and come back to remind me of our agreement. But he didn't. How was I ever going to get Bud to say he was protecting the casino? It was a long weekend, and I did not go to Bud's bar as I usually did on Saturday or Sunday. I did not know what to say to Bud. I certainly did not want him to tell me he and his crew quit. I had worked to damn hard to get us where we are.

On Monday, Bud unexpectedly showed up at my shop. I brought him back to my office and with the camera rolling and recorded his every word.

"I'm pissed that me and my crew were not paid. That was not the deal," Bud said. And at that, he pulled out his badge, "Our agreement was you pay for the tin. You are not just paying for the night we work. You are paying for me and my guys who are working through the week gathering intelligence to make sure no one is looking or interested in your game. Therefore, you owe me and my guys our money, and I want it today, or we're done."

My heart started to race with excitement. Did that really just happen? Did I really get him on tape saying he was not only protecting the casino but also gathering intelligence to make sure no one is looking at our game? There must have been someone watching over me. There must be a God. I could not believe what just happened. Elation, I believe, would be the best word to describe how I felt at that very moment. I could not wait to tell Bob and Dan.

"I understand. I will get you your money," I assured Bud.

"You have until the end of today," he replied, making sure I knew he was in charge.

"Okay," I said. "I will have it by the end of the day."

Bud left, and I called Dan. We had a meeting later that day, and I played the videotape Dan and Bob were delighted. Alleluia! I got the money and called Bud to come back to the shop, and on camera, Bud and I together counted out all the money and identified which police officer was getting paid as I handed the counted money over to Bud.

♥ ♥ ♥

I had made good on my payment to Bud. But someone must have gotten suspicious. I got a call from Mr. Paxton saying that someone from the Cleveland Police Department called requesting information on my employment. Mr. Paxton provided them with the exact information we had collectively put together as part of my background before I started the operation. The information was that I had worked there from 1985 thru early 1989 as a sales representative and that I left to open a business up north somewhere in Ohio. Mr. Paxton did a great job, and I thanked him profusely. Preparation is so important for an undercover agent.

CHAPTER

After a successful night, and my big scare, I decided I would head home, surprise everyone as it had been weeks since I had been home. I arrived home around 1 am, after another round of evasive driving techniques.

I was glad to be home. I felt like this was the first time I would be able to have some quality time with my family. Even if it was only for a day. I pressed the button on my garage door opener, and it began to rise. Inside was a new silver Chrysler Mini-Van. I almost threw up. *Where was my 1987 Oldsmobile Cutlass Supreme with spoke wheels?* I got out of my car and inspected the Mini-Van. I walked outside and checked the address just to be sure I was in the right house. Yep, it was my house, but whose Mini-Van and where was my 1987 Oldsmobile Cutlass Supreme?

I was fuming. Lynn was already in bed, sound asleep. "Who's mini-van is that in the garage?" I asked, spitting my words.

"It's ours. I just bought it," she said flatly.

I was so upset that I just turned around and left. "How could she do that?" I sputtered my entire drive back to my undercover apartment. My beautiful Cutlass Supreme with spoke wheels was gone. "How could she do that?"

I realized later that she was able to do this because I was never home and rarely listened to her. But there wasn't much I could do about it. I was gone, and so was the Cutlass Supreme.

I had to pick up the money from either Dan or Rick sometime before the casino opened Friday afternoon. I was given a duffle bag that contained $25,000 in cash. I would then run the casino from about 9:00 pm until 9:00 am Saturday. After everyone had left, I would drive to my undercover apartment and meet with whoever was working the cameras that night. I would hand over the audiotapes and the money from the casino. When I returned the money, I would have close to $40,000.

This was creating an unforeseen problem in my under-cover operation. Usually, the funding for such an operation would be spent on buying stolen property, drugs, bribes/payoffs. Operations rarely made money. SHIRON was making a lot of money every week. Not only was I generating profits from the casino, but my Tee-Shirt shop was also making money, and we did not know what to do with all the money we were generating from the operation. So, we were simply putting all this money in the SAC's safe.

Numerous discussions between DOJ, FBIHQ, and Cleveland FBI determined that the best way to address this unique problem. The DOJ came up with a guideline that allowed profits made in an undercover operation to be utilized in the operation to offset certain expenses. There were specific instances identified when and how the money could be spent. The money could be used to pay rent for the tee-shirt shop and materials, utilities, or other items that would usually be paid out of our budget. We could not use that money to pay off the police officers.

♥ ♥ ♥

March 1990

There are always unexpected events that throw the case in a new direction. Typically, arrests are big triggers. And that was the same for us. Benny was arrested. Benny was our first informant, and he knew I was with the FBI. He also knew that I caught him lying, and I was the reason he was removed from the operation. It was no surprise Benny found himself in trouble with the law again. It was his M.O. But now he was sitting in the jail where Bud worked. And of course, he was going to do and say anything he could to get out of that cell.

Benny tells the arresting officer that he is working for the FBI and that he needs to speak with Special Agent Dan Estrem immediately. The police officer called Dan to verify the story. Dan showed up at the Cleveland City Jail twenty minutes later. Bud greeted him.

"You Special Agent Estrem?" Bud asked, curious.

"I am. Please place Benny Grant into a private interrogation room for me to speak with him?" Dan said flatly.

Benny sat handcuffed at a table. Dan sat down across

from him. "Listen to me very closely. Do not say another word. I will take care of this. If you say anything to anyone about the job you were doing, I will no longer use you as an informant. Do you understand?"

Benny agreed. Dan paid Benny handsomely for his work, and Benny did not want to lose his monthly payments from Dan. Benny might have been a little slow, but he knew where his bread was buttered. Benny now understood the situation he just created was not a good one. But the damage had been done.

Dan left Benny sitting in jail. Bud, the curious one, had questions.

"Agent Estrem. What is it that guy does for you?" Bud asked.

"Domestic terrorism matters," Dan said, flatly. He knew he had to give Bud something as Bud's next stop was the bar where I would eventually see him later that night.

Unaware of Benny's antics, that evening, I was headed for Walt's Café. I was approximately three to four blocks away when I got a page. I looked at the page. I saw it was Dan. "I'll just call him later when I am done at Walt's Café," I muttered to myself. But then, for some reason, I reconsidered and stopped at a payphone to call Dan.

When I got ahold of Dan, I could sense that he was agitated and nervous. Dan asked, "Where are you?"

"I am heading to Walt's Café."

Dan said, "You can't go."

"Why?" I asked.

Dan laid out to me what had happened. I said, "Dan, I have to go as I was supposed to meet with Bud regarding a Darts tournament."

Dan again explained what had happened at the jail, and stated, "You can't go to Walt's Café tonight we just heard on the wire that he thinks you're a fed."

"Are you sure?" I asked.

"Yes. His bar, home, and jail are all bugged. I have been listening to the tapes."

I thought for a moment and told Dan, "If I don't go, he'll know I'm a fed. I'll take off the recorder and take it back to my office, so even if they check my car it'll be clean."

Dan agreed. "Call me as soon as you get out of there." I did as we discussed and headed back to Walt's Café. Normally when I used to walk into Walt's Cafe, I got the same reaction Norm used to get when he walked into Cheers. Everyone would yell, "Ray," and I would go around the bar, greeting everyone. But not today.

The bar was completely silent. No cheerful greetings. No smiles. The jukebox wasn't even playing some loud, obnoxious song. Nothing. No one said a word. Complete silence. My adrenaline started pumping, and I needed to calm myself down as I knew I was about to be searched. Sitting at the bar closest to the door was a big burly guy I had never seen before. As soon as I walked in, Bud nodded his head to the big beefy guy. The guy stood up and approached me. I tried to avoid him and walked in the other direction towards where Bill was seated. This big guy was fast on his feet and was able to intercept me before I could get to Bill. Before I could say anything, the guy envelops me with his massive arms and barrel chest acting as though he is drunk and begins to feel me up and down.

I wanted him to search me and search me good, so he

can assure Bud that I was not wearing a wire. But I can't just let him do it without getting pissed and trying to avoid it.

I begin to fight back and attempt to push him away all the time, letting him get as good a feel as he can. "Check here, why don't you?" I said, taking his hand and placing it on my crotch. "What the hell is going on, Bud?" I asked, pretending to be furious.

"Ah, he's drunk, don't mind him," Bud tells me, and then addresses the burly man, "Let him go." Thank God Dan had paged me. If he hadn't, the case would have been over, and we were just getting started. I walked over to Bud and said, what was that all about? Bud shrugged it off, saying ah, "he doesn't know you, and that's his way of saying hello." I just said that's an idiotic way to do it, and you should do something about it.

CHAPTER

22

I continued running the casino and the Tee-shirt shop for several more weeks. Through my nightly rounds at the various bars and clubs, I met a Joe Pesci look-a-like who went by the name of Russell the Muscle. Russell was a wannabe cop. He spoke the lingo and dressed the part. But in actuality, he was a licensed Private Detective who didn't have much business. He lived in his office, which was a dirty, dingy place that rarely had any electricity because he could not afford it. Once in a while, he would have running water, but more often than not, he didn't have that either.

Russell smoked constantly, never stopped talking or walking. Russell spoke as if he just arrived from the Bronx. But Russell did have a lot of 'cop friends,' so he said. Russell hung out mostly at the Cleveland Police Patrolmen's Association (CPPA), which was a nice bar, game room, and lounge for all Cleveland Police officers. The head of the CPPA was a man by the name of Karl Spokes.

Dan had heard that Karl was dirty and worked him for

quite some time, but nothing ever came of it. Russell was a good friend of Karl's. When Dan heard that I was getting close to Russell he immediately started to focus my efforts on getting close to Karl.

Karl was a Cleveland Police Officer, as well as the head of the CPPA. He was approximately 5' 11" and was a solid brick wall. Karl was power-hungry leach who used his position and his close friends to get whatever he wanted.

Karl tended to want to dominate and control others regardless of the situation. Karl often took advantage of those around him. I believed he used Russell in this manner as well. However, I wasn't above taking advantage of the lechery.

Karl felt superior to others, and that was why he had no issues with taking kickbacks from anyone who did business with him. Karl believed that with his position came entitlements, and he took advantage of every opportunity that presented itself.

I worked Russell for several weeks before I even brought up Karl's name. I went as far as to hire Russell as a sales representative for my Tee-shirt shop, knowing that his first client would most likely be Karl and the CPPA.

Russell set up a meeting with Karl and brought me down to the CPPA for the meeting. As we were driving to the meeting, Russell kept talking about all the items we could sell to the CPPA tee-shirts, jackets, hats, sweatshirts, sweatpants, softball uniforms. Russell's eyes were lighting up just thinking of the bonus he was going to receive for the contract we were going to get with the CPPA.

The CPPA was a large two-story brick building that includes a large bar area, game room, and dance floor. It also houses the offices of the presiding officers to include the President of the CPPA. We met Karl in his office, which was on the second floor of the CPAA office on West 58th Street.

I sat down at the round table with Karl, Russell, Karl's secretary Marissa. I presented all the things my company could make for the CPPA. I worked Karl like I was a true salesman. I allowed Karl to finagle the price and showed him all the products, pushing for a big sale.

"Write it up and give me a final cost," Karl said like a proud lion.

The CPPA had just contracted an order for over $15,000 worth of merchandise that included softball uniforms, hats, jackets, bat bags, and tee shirts for the CPPA. I had no idea how much this was going to cost me, but I got the order. Now I just had to wait for the shakedown from Karl.

I went back to my shop and wrote out the order. The next day I showed the order to Russell. Russell nearly came to tears as I had promised him a bonus of 6% of the total order. Russell was about to make $900.00. He had not made that much money at any one time in his life. Russell delivered the order sheet to the CPPA. Now all I had to do was wait.

The next day Russell came bounding into my office, cigarette in hand, and talking as fast as an auctioneer. I flipped on the switch for the video camera that was in my desk drawer and asked him to slow down and tell me what he was trying to say. "I went to see Karl this morning. The deal is on. But Karl wants $1,500 for making the deal. And he wants $500 for his secretary."

"Why would I have to pay him $1,500 for making an order with me?"

Russell gave me a look as if I had three heads and said, "Because that's how we do business."

"Not where I'm from," I replied.

Russell started to get agitated and said, "That's how Karl does business. He just did you a big favor and wants a little something in return."

"Okay. But why should I have to give Marissa any money?" I asked.

"Because Karl is having an affair with her and likes to keep her happy."

"Is Marissa a police officer?"

"Yes, and she is also married to a police officer."

I was now about to bust Russell's bubble. "Russell, they are both cops, and you are asking me to make payoffs to two cops for doing business with the CPPA, a police organization. Are you nuts?"

Russell started walking around the room a little faster, and his smoking increased significantly. He said, "You are not going to get arrested! They asked for the money."

"So, you're telling me, the fact that they asked for the money means I won't have any problems?"

"Absolutely!"

"How am I supposed to do this? I am not just going to walk in his office and hand him $2,000?"

"No," Russell said almost indignantly as if I had no payoff etiquette.

"You will get two envelopes. Mark one with a K and put $1,500 into that envelope. That's Karl's. The second envelope you mark with an M and put $500 in that envelope that's Marissa's. When we walk into Karl's office, you hand him the envelopes, and he will hand you a check for $15,000 to pay for the CPPA order. It's that simple," Russell said.

Just to hear it one more time and to get on videotape for a second time, I said, "I don't know Russell. This is making me very nervous. Tell me again exactly what Karl said to you, and you better not be lying to me."

Russell explained it one more time.

"Okay, come back tomorrow, and I will have the money, and we can take the money over to Karl."

I waited for Russell to leave and then called Dan from a payphone (I always called Dan or Rick or anyone from the FBI from a payphone) and told him we needed to meet. I grabbed the tape that just memorialized this conversation from the recorder.

We met at my undercover apartment, and I put the tape in pushed play and nothing but fuzz. Nothing was recorded. Dan looked at me, and I looked back at him. I felt as if my blood had just rushed out of my body. I must have turned pale. I explained to Dan what should have been on the videotape.

"You have to get him to repeat it," he said.

"I can't. Why can't I just do an FD 302 explaining what was said and then note that there was a malfunction of the recorder? We do that all of the time."

"Not with Karl. We have to get Russell to repeat it."

My blood was boiling. How the hell could this have happened? That was, without a doubt, one of the best recordings I had done to date, and I had nothing to show for it. Who could or even would possibly want to explain that all again?

Dan and I went over what could have happened to cause

the recorder to malfunction. A video recorder and camera were hidden in my office. A camera strategically hidden in the room allowed me to secretly record any conversation in my office. The ceiling was a drop ceiling with panels that allowed access to the recorder.

The bookcase was on the back wall behind and to the right of my desk. There was a small couch on the wall opposite my desk directly in front of the hidden camera. The door to my office was right in front of my desk. This allowed me to see from the shop area to the front door. From my desk, I had a clear line of sight of the shop, which allowed me to identify whoever was entering the shop quickly.

In my top right-hand desk drawer, I had a remote control that the Tech Agents had set up to remotely turn the video camera on just by pushing the button. The same as when you open your garage door from your car. Therefore, if I saw one of the subjects entering the shop, I could simply reach into my top right-hand drawer to push the button, and the recorder would begin to record. There was also a microphone covertly installed to record the conversation if I had to step out of my office but wanted to continue to record the conversation. The front part of the shop also had video capability that was operated remotely with a remote control. It had worked so many times before. What could have gone wrong this time?

After a lengthy discussion of what could have happened, we decided the batteries in the remote control must be dead. The next day when I arrived at the shop, I changed the batteries, stood on my chair, and lifted the ceiling panel so I could see if the red light on the recorder came on when I pushed the remote. It did. Problem fixed!

I then called Russell and asked him to stop by the shop. When Russell arrived, I asked him to sit down on the couch that was facing the camera. To get Russell to sit was a monumental task in and of itself. Russell loved to pace while he smoked and talked. I then told Russell that he had not convinced me that paying a kickback to Karl for the contract with the CPPA was a good idea. I knew I had to get the words kickback, Karl, contract, and CPPA in the recorded conversation to satisfy the AUSA, Bob.

Russell started to get agitated and said again, "That this is the way Karl does business he does something for you, and you do something for him."

"But what did Karl do for me?" I asked. I needed Russell to say he gave you a $15,000 contract. And that he did.

Russell went on to say, "If he did not give the contract to you, he would have given it to someone else, and they would be paying him the $1,500."

"And I also pay Marissa the $500.00?"

"Hell, yes," was Russell's response.

So far, so good. "Russell, can you explain to me again what Karl said about how he wants to paid?" I thought Russell was going to choke on his spit. He was so angry.

"Are you fucking nuts? Are you some kind of idiot? Do you not have a brain?" This, coming from a guy who lived in his office with no heat, water, or job. I responded I just want to make sure I got this right. You are asking me to pay a kickback to a police officer on a contract with a Police organization.

Russell exasperated as he could be explained the entire process again. After Russell had finished, I said: "Okay, let's get this done tomorrow."

Russell left happy but still disappointed that the deal was not yet done, and he had not yet received his $900.00 bonus. After Russell had left, I turned off the recorder and went up in the ceiling to retrieve the videotape from the recorder.

I called Dan and informed him that I had the tape, and I was able to get Russell to state the facts all over again. "Did you check to make sure the remote worked as well?" Dan asked.

"I checked it several times before Russell stopped by."

"Good. We'll meet you at the apartment to pick up the tapes."

When I opened the door to my apartment to let Dan in standing there with Dan was Bob, Rick, and Herb. After our initial hellos, I put the tape in and sat back, waiting to see all my guests smile and nod enthusiastically at the video.

To my great surprise, the tape was once again blank— Nada, nothing, zero, nothing but fuzz and static. None of my guests smiled, nor were any of them enthusiastic. Puzzled and dismayed was more like it. *Now, what went wrong?*

"Are you sure you checked the recorder to make sure it came on when you hit the remote?" Dan asked.

"I am positive."

At this point, I suggested we have our tech agents go in and check to see what is going on. That night our tech agents covertly entered my shop. They found that the wire that ran from the camera to the recorder had gotten loose and fallen down behind the wall. They fixed it immediately, and I was back in business. But now I had to go through the entire process of getting Russell to state the plan on tape for the third time. I thought there is no way he is going to do this again. But then again, he was looking forward to that $900.

I called Russell and started the rigamarole again. Russell was pissed. "Are you a fucking idiot?" he yelled.

"No, Russell. I am just very nervous and want to make sure I am clear and that no one is setting me up. And if you want your money, you'll explain to me one more time why I have to pay a kickback to a police officer for a simple $15,000 contract and that you and Karl are not setting me up. Angry as hell, Russell explained it one more time.

After checking the tapes and making sure everything was clear, I made the payoffs, and Russell got his $900.00 and was able to get some heat and water in his office. And the CPPA got some great tee-shirts, jackets, hats, bat bags, and softball uniforms.

I used a tiny Panasonic microcassette recorder to capture all of my conversations. It was a small device that had a wire that ran up the shirt and was taped in the middle of my chest. And although it was small and could fit in my pocket, it caused a rather conspicuous bulge. We needed to find a place to hide the device that wouldn't be seen. I initially tried to conceal my recorder in those hideous cowboy boots, but not only did I not like the boots, but the recorder was also unable to pick up a lot of the conversation. I then tried to keep the microphone in taped to my leg. But then I found that if I sat down, which I did quite often at the bars, the receiver was unable to pick up the conversations as well. After playing around, I found that if I tucked the recorder into my crotch that I was able to keep the microphone in my shirt plus when it came to a general pat-down, typically, no one wanted to touch another man's crotch.

Two weeks after my deal with Karl, I got a call from Bud's girlfriend, Karen. Karen lived in an apartment above Walt's Café with Bud. She worked as a bartender and played manager when Bud was away. She was a pretty lady, tall and slender with brown hair and brown eyes. Karen struck me as well educated and well-traveled. I couldn't figure out why she was hanging around with the likes of Bud. Karen and I developed a close, friendly, trusting relationship and would talk often when I was at Walt's Café. Again, as I learned from Donnie Brasco, get close to those who are close to your main target.

"What's up, Karen?" I asked. Her call made me nervous. The last thing I wanted was for Bud to think I was stepping over some line or something.

"I shouldn't be doing this, but..." she paused.

"But?" I asked, prompting her.

"I feel like you are on the up and up, and you deserve to know," sounding hesitant.

"Know what?" I asked, hoping she would continue.

"But is going to call you later today and ask you to come to the bar. Karl was in last night, and he was drunk and started to complain to Bud about the fact that he doesn't like the deal you made with him. And Karl told Bud he thinks you're a fed. It is making Bud doubt who you are," she said, her words lined with fear.

"Karen, I am who I say I am. I have been loyal to Bud since I met him. I have made good on everything I said. And, I didn't want to pay Karl a kickback. He insisted.

Maybe now Karl is worried he made a mistake and is trying to blame me."

"I know. That is why I thought you should know. Please don't tell him I called you," she hung up the phone without a goodbye.

I informed Dan of the call from Karen and let him know that when I got the call from Bud, I was not going to wear my recorder as I was sure Bud would want to search me. Dan agreed. We'll make it clear in our 302 he said.

About one hour later, I got a call from Bud. I went down to the bar.

"Hey Bud," I said, giving him a wave and pretending I thought it was a friendly visit.

"Who are you, Ray? Who are you really?" he asked.

"What? What are you talking about?"

"You came out of nowhere? I mean, what do we know about you?" Bud said.

"Seriously?! Bud, we have been working together for more than six months you have known me for almost a year. I am not a fed, and I am not wearing a wire." If that is what you are asking.

I then unbuttoned my shirt and started to pull down my pants when Bud stopped me and said, "I know you're not a fed, but Karl and I go way back, and I just wanted to show him that he has nothing to be afraid of."

"I have paid you a lot of money, and you have done some good work for me. But this is the second time you have challenged me about this, and quite frankly, I am not going to put up with it any longer. One more time and I will not need your services anymore."

"I get it, man," Bud said, apologizing and taking back his accusation.

"We good?" I asked.

"We are," he said, extending his hand to me. I shook his hand and walked out the door.

During the operation, I was searched for a wire eleven times. Eight of those times, I was wearing the recorder, and they did not find it. As I said, no one wanted to check my crotch. But I also made it hard for them to search me. I would continuously fidget; sometimes, I would act angry and push them away. Whatever it took and depending on who it was, determined how I would play that. Of the three times, I was not wearing a wire it was because I made a conscious decision to do so. Another lesson from Donnie Brasco.

CHAPTER

23

May 1990

We were thirteen months into the investigation. I had held over twenty-five games and paid twelve police officers for protecting an illegal gambling operation. Things were rolling, and I was in deep. I was no longer Ray Morrow FBI Agent but Brad Ray Morgan. Any semblance of my real life was gone. And the last thing I wanted was to be pulled away from the case for any reason. But the FBI had protocols, and one of those rules was frequent psychological testing. And as May came to a close, I was sent to Quantico for my evaluation.

I knew I was in denial, telling myself things were okay. That I was doing the right thing, but deep down, I knew that personally, things were not so good. Lynn had been telling me for months that I was 'gone' and that I had 'changed.' But when you are in too deep, you are the last one to see it. I was not paying attention to what I was doing unless it concerned the operation. But as I said before, if you are doing it right, the undercover operation will consume you, and it did.

I am not proud of the decisions I made regarding my family. I was so engaged in the case that I made the decision not to attend my son Ross' First Holy Communion service. I did not want a subject to see me attending someone's First Holy Communion. I couldn't explain that. My undercover persona had no family or friends in the area. Why would I be there? I had no plausible excuse, or so I thought.

I remember my first communion so well. Taking the biscuit. My mom and dad were watching me receive my First Holy Communion. And there I was not attending the communion of my eldest son. I felt horrible. A pit erupted in my stomach. At the last moment, I decided I would go to the church. I would never forgive myself if I missed this event. When I arrived, I parked quite a distance from the church and walked to the church. When I got inside the church, I saw there was a balcony section and went there to observe. As soon as Ross received his First Holy Communion, I left. No one knew I was there. It was like I had become a ghost. There was a party at our house, several of my relatives had driven in from Western Pennsylvania to celebrate, and I did not attend that either. I just didn't want to ruin Ross' big day, and I was positive that my being there would have created some animosity from Lynn, who busted her ass to pull this whole thing off. I figured it was better if I wasn't there.

I missed every one of my boys' little league games. I did try to attend a few of them, but I would sit on a hill far away from the baseball fields and watch. I was so far away from the baseball fields that I wasn't even sure which ones were my sons. I decided it wasn't worth risking the investigation for a game.

While all this was happening, I thought it was okay to do this. I thought I'm merely protecting my family and the integrity of the investigation. It wasn't until later after everything was over that I realized how wrong I was.

However, Lynn started to say exactly that to me whenever I came home, which became more and more infrequent. Because when I was home, all she did was point out the obvious, and I didn't want to see or hear the truth. I had much more important things to think about and consider.

"What's wrong with you? You've changed. You don't seem to care about us anymore."

"I haven't changed, you just don't understand or care about what I'm going through," I would tell her, trying to control my anger.

But she was right. I started to become less trusting, my family was no longer my primary interest or priority, and I found that I could only focus on one thing. My passion solely focused on just one thing, and that was the operation.

I became very lonely and distant from my friends and relatives during this time. I just knew that anyone not involved in the operation could not possibly understand what I was going through. I stopped going to church during the operation. I became very guarded and would not let anyone get close to me. I was no longer the fun-loving, gregarious individual I use to be. I did not want to socialize with anyone outside of the operation. I only wanted to work on the subjects, and when I met with Dan, Rick, Herb, or Bob, I just wanted to talk about the operation. Nothing else mattered to me. And while Lynn was the first to recognize this and tried so hard to get me to see the truth, I couldn't. I just kept thinking how selfish of her.

I thought the case is going great. I'm doing great. It must be Lynn. She was the problem, not me. I am positive now that most of what I said and thought was because of the operation, but some of it was because I did not want to hear what Lynn had to say. I had more important things to do.

One day I got a message to come home as soon as possible. When I arrived, Lynn was putting my sons in that godforsaken Mini-Van.

"I am leaving. I am taking the boys. We are going home to live with my mother and father."

I didn't argue. I am not sure if she thought I would. I simply said, "okay."

At this point, the case was more important; it was the most important thing in my world. Somehow, I justified that and let the best things that ever happened to me walk out the door. Or should I say drive away in a Chrysler Mini-Van? I truly hated that car.

I told no one about this. Not Dan, not Rick, not Herb. I was fine, or at least I thought I was. Nothing was going to stop me. This was several weeks before my scheduled psychological testing and interview with Steve Band. I took the test as usual. No problem, I thought I have this down.

A few hours after taking the tests, I went for my follow up interview. I knew I had this. I would wrap up the interview and be back on the road to Cleveland within hours.

I walked into Steve's office, and Steve said to me, "Ray, what's wrong?"

I said nothing.

"Tell me what's been bothering you."

"Steve, I am fine. The case is moving along just fine, and things are going well."

Steve looked at me and said, "Ray, you are tighter than a drum. Your tests are off the chart. Way off of your base scores. If you don't tell me what is going on. I will have to remove you from the case because you are about to explode."

I thought that damn test. I was sure I had answered it the way I always did. But I didn't.

Steve looked at me and said, "What's going on?

I broke down and started sobbing and told Steve what had happened at home with my wife and kids. Steve knew through our many conversations how much I loved my wife and my children. When I finished, Steve looked at me and said, "Do you have a car here?"

"Yes, I drove down from Cleveland."

"I want you to get in your car and drive back to Pittsburgh and see your family. Take some time to spend with them, but you need to get them back into your life. You are falling apart. I'll let Cleveland know that I just wanted you to take some time off. I'll tell them you need a break."

I was still crying, but a fantastic feeling came over me. Steve was right. I needed my family. I loved them way too much to lose them. How did I let this get so out of hand?

I showed up at my in-laws' door and fell into Lynn's arms. I was so relieved that she was gracious enough to allow me to come back.

"I have sacrificed so much for your dream. I have done

RAY A. MORROW WITH LINDSAY PRESTON

it happily, and you let us down," she said, her eyes filled with tears.

"I promise you it won't happen again," I said, my eyes welling over.

"No, it won't." She said.

"I won't even go back to Cleveland if you don't want me to," I said, hoping she wouldn't take me up on the offer.

And she didn't. She knew me too well. She knew I was remorseful but also knew I had a job to do.

"Go back. Finish up. We will be here when you are done." I thought to myself, man, I love her. If I were her, I would have left me a long time ago and never looked back. But here she was graciously taking me back. On my ride back to Cleveland, I remember listening to Bob Seger's "It's You" over and over again:

"Just about the time I think I've had it
Everything I've planned has fallen through
Just about the time the whole thing's crumbling in
And I can't hold back no matter what I do
And just about the time, I feel like screaming
And finding me a wall to punch right through
I look up, and I just can't help smiling
It's You"

♥ ♥ ♥

When I got back to Cleveland, I felt like a huge boulder had been lifted off my chest and was relieved that my personal life was back on track, be it a slow track. And even though my family was living in Pittsburgh while I worked in Cleveland, the deep love and respect Lynn and I had for one another was working its way back into our lives. We both understood what we had to do to keep our family together and to get through this exceedingly difficult and challenging time. We both knew what we wanted, and both agreed to do our best to support one another.

I didn't know how I let my life slip so far from my grasps. How did it happen? Where did it all go wrong? But the answer was simple; it was me. I realized on my drive back to Cleveland that Lynn was right, I had changed and not for the better. This was the first time I could not leave my work at the office, so to speak. I carried it with me, and I rationalized all my bad decisions because I knew that she didn't understand. Quite frankly, only those who have worked deep undercover could understand. I had read DONNIE BRASCO and thought I knew what to expect. But the reality was a completely different animal that; it is impossible to grasp the magnitude of its hold on you. In my case, the person who knew me best recognized it and tried to tell me time and time again, I just would not believe her. A mistake I promised myself, I would never make again.

209

CHAPTER

24

SHIRON - the third six months – June 1990

I returned to Cleveland to kick off the third six months of
SHIRON. I was starting to recruit other police officers and
had over 15 police officers working for my gambling operation. The number of gamblers and attendees had increased
so much that we had to move to a larger facility. My FBI
team and I decided to make a move from the west side of
Cleveland to the east side.

Dan found a large warehouse on St. Clair Avenue on the
East Side of Cleveland that could house the casino and was
able to park all of the gambler's cars inside. That was a massive perk that the players loved. It always looked suspicious
having dozens of cars parked outside my tee-shirt shop at
three, four, or five in the morning. This new facility would
eliminate this one risk.

The front of the warehouse had a vast open area where
I would set up the casino. In the back were several offices,
which were near the entrance of the garage. My new office

was much bigger than the one on the West Side. My desk was on the back wall across from the bookcase, which again housed one of the cameras in my office. Along the opposite wall, there was a small credenza and a few chairs on each side of the credenza. The front door to the main office area always remained locked. I insisted everyone enter through the garage door. It was the best way of keeping tabs on who was coming and going.

Our tech agents, the wires and pliers' guys, went to work installing cameras and microphones throughout the facility. They covered every inch of that location with video cameras and microphones. In my office, they built a bookcase behind my desk. Strategically, hidden in my office was a camera that could record everything that happened. They installed cameras in the front part of the building where the casino would be. They placed cameras in the garage area. Cameras and audio recorders covered the entire facility. The video recorders were hidden up in a loft above the garage area under lock and key in a cabinet the tech agents had built. This place was twice the size as my old location, and we needed it as my casino was becoming a very popular destination.

A few weeks after we had rented the warehouse, I got a call from Herm Groman, an undercover agent in Detroit, Michigan. Herm had been down to my undercover operation several times, acting like a big-time gambler from Detroit.

"Would you be interested in $250,000 worth of original GM auto parts? They were being used in another operation in Detroit that had been working with GM regarding fake

GM auto parts. The operation has been shut down, and they weren't needed anymore. FBI granted permission for them to be used in another operation. Would you like to house them in your warehouse? Tell people they are stolen items?" Herm asked.

I thought about it for a moment. That might be a good play. It would make me seem like an even more legit criminal. "Absolutely, thanks, Herm."

A few days later, my warehouse was filled with genuine GM auto parts. They were quite the conversation starter. Everyone asked me if they were stolen or for sale. I told people that I was holding them for a friend until the heat died down. They made for great props and helped to make me seem like a perfect bad guy.

● ● ●

July 1990

We ran the casino for three more weeks with Bud's crew, but they were getting more and more dangerous and flamboyant. Earl Whitman, one of Bud's most trusted crew members, was becoming a problem. Earl was approximately 6′ tall and weighed nearly 190 pounds. He was a solid brick wall and looked almost as crazy as he was. Earl was a veteran of the Cleveland Police Officer and was absolutely unstable and unpredictable. Earl drank excessively, was usually drunk on duty, and, while on duty, would often go to whorehouses and spend the majority of his shift there.

One particular evening, he was working my casino while simultaneously working his police shift. Earl, dressed in his police blues, would leave periodically throughout the night to cover his patrol sector. He would patrol his area and circle back each hour to check on the casino. He did this the entire night. Just as the night was ending, and the sun was beginning to rise, Earl pulled his police cruiser into the warehouse, sirens blaring, light flashing, laughing and drunk out of his mind. He scared the shit out of me and all my gamblers. Earl was a loose cannon, and I wasn't sure how far he would end up going.

The following Friday night, as I was driving to the East Side warehouse for our casino night, I received a page from Bud. I called him immediately.

"Meet me at the Holiday Inn on Rockside Road in Cleveland."

"What's going on? I need to get to the warehouse."

"Just meet me. Meet me in the lobby. It won't take long."

I got off at the next exit. Did a U-turn and headed towards the Holiday Inn. I had no idea what I was walking into. I pulled into a parking spot as close to the front door as I could. I wasn't sure if this was a trap. It didn't make sense. Why wouldn't Bud just meet me at my warehouse office? I walked towards the conference room and slowly opened the door. Bud was there, along with Earl.

Earl had frequent and sudden mood shifts. Whenever things were not going Earl's way, he would often blame everyone around him. Earl's emotions would explode unexpectedly, and he would become angry or self-destructive with his actions. He was literally a ticking time bomb, and I never knew what to expect from Earl. His presence made me even warier of this entire meeting.

"Why couldn't we just meet at the warehouse?" I asked Bud.

"We got a call from a friend in vice tonight. We were told that the warehouse is being watched, and a raid is planned for tonight. They are sitting on the warehouse right now, just waiting for us to arrive," Bud said. Earl was nodding in confirmation to his story.

"Are you sure?" I asked.

"Sure, as shit," Earl barked.

"I have to make some calls. I need to let the dealers and gamblers know that we are not playing tonight and to stay away from the warehouse."

"Don't tell them why," Bud ordered.

I nodded and left the hotel. I immediately called Dan and informed him of the news. "That is fantastic. Just fantastic." He paused. "You did record that, right?"

"Yes, I did."

The next day Bud and Earl showed up at my Tee-shirt shop.

"Hey, guys," I said, trying not to sound nervous. I didn't like that they were there unexpectedly.

Earl moved his jacket aside, showing me that he was packing. I pretended not to notice.

"Is there a problem?" I ask.

"Were just making sure that next week's game is going to be on and that you didn't fuck up and tell the gamblers what went down," Bud said.

"You came down to ask me that in person?" I replied.

"Just answer the question," Earl ordered.

"It is on. And I didn't say anything."

"Good," Bud replied. "That's all. We'll see you next week."

With that, they left. But I knew now that things were out of hand with Bud and his crew. They were dangerous. It wouldn't be hard for them to raid my place and steal all the money and kill me. And they were not above doing it. Earl was the groups' collector, and I had heard stories of him doing drive-by shootings at the homes of people who owed the crew money. A cop doing drive-by shootings on innocent families! The man was insane!

I made Dan and Rick aware of this, and we decided to move on from the crew. I called Bud a few days later and told him that I had gotten information that the casino was still being watched, and for ALL of our safety, I was going to shut down the casino until I knew it was safe to proceed. After much apprehension, he agreed. I started to pursue other leads and develop unwitting informants aggressively. I was very leery at this point of going any further with Bud and his crew. We needed to move on. But how?

CHAPTER

25

Late July 1990

Moving on from Bud's crew required me to find new targets. And new targets required new introductions. On July 18, I was introduced to Reggie Hughes by another of Dan's informants. Reggie was an African American who worked as a bail bondsman. Reggie was a former police officer who knew just about everyone in the Cleveland law enforcement and judicial arenas.

Reggie was a wheeler-dealer and was into just nearly everything from stolen property to drug dealing. Reggie was an extremely likable man, that could have been a stand-up comedian. I enjoyed my time around Reggie, but I was also always on edge because he was so unpredictable. Reggie went 100 miles an hour all the time. Reggie used cocaine often, and that made him a little unstable at times and, at those times, caused me great consternation.

Reggie had a problem staying focused. The slightest distraction, and he lost his train of thought. Despite this,

Reggie always thought he was the smartest, most important guy in the room. I was not as confident in Reggie as he was. But even so, I became close with Reggie and slowly began to tell him all about me, not the real me, the undercover me.

From our conversations, Reggie learned of my gambling operation, and I also slowly let him learn of my supposed background in marijuana dealing. Reggie quickly introduced me to some of his friends in the police department who would be interested in protecting my gambling operation.

Reggie took a chug of his beer. "I also have some judge friends that I can introduce you to. They may be willing to help protect you as well."

"Really? Judges?" I asked. This could be fantastic. Dan would be thrilled if we could follow this up the ladder. "Let's do it!"

"It will cost ya. I can't afford charity work. You get that, right?" Reggie asked. Nothing was free with Reggie, so I wasn't surprised. But I had no problem paying Reggie because he earned it. When Reggie said he was going to do something, he did it. You just had to keep up with him.

"I need a new place to set up the casino until I feel it's safe to go back to the warehouse. Would you want to help me locate a new place?" I asked him.

I needed to stay away from the warehouse for a while longer until I was sure that Bud's crew did not think we were running the games anymore. Also, I wanted to wait a while to make sure the police weren't still watching the warehouse. I was trying to lay low, as they say, regarding the casino, but Reggie wanted some of that money we had talked about protecting the casino. "Sure thing, Ray. I got you covered," Reggie replied. Reggie was working every angle he could to get paid.

♥ ♥ ♥

A few days later, I got a call, Reggie. "Meet me at my office. I have something I need to tell you. It's big." Reggie's Bail Bond Office was next to the Cleveland Municipal Courthouse.

"I will be there in 20." I wired up and drove down to his office. I parked my car and walked down the street to Reggie's office.

"Ray! Ray!" Reggie was standing on the steps of the courthouse yelling to me. "Come over here," he shouted, waving at me.

I walked across the street, and before I can even greet Reggie, he starts blabbering, "Get this. We are going to meet one of the judges I was telling you about. I had dinner with her last night and laid out your marijuana operation, and she's willing to help! We are going upstairs to meet her now!"

I started to walk up the stairs. I was filled with excitement. *Wait until Dan hears about this! What a huge score!*

I pulled open the oversized metal doors of the courthouse. The place was grand. Stone from floor to ceiling. It was a beautiful piece of architecture with massive pillars more than suitable for a house of justice. My fascination with the building passed quickly when I stood face to face with a magnetometer I was going to have to pass through. I had my little Panasonic recorder in my crotch. That was absolutely going to set the thing off. I was going to ding like I was packing. *How am I going to explain that?*

Oh shit! I was about to blow the entire operation. This little recorder has almost done me in over a dozen times, and this time it seems it may have gotten me. *Think!*

I pulled Reggie to the side and said, "Reggie, I can't go in there and talk to a judge about doing something illegal."

Reggie said, "She is waiting for you."

We kept walking towards the magnetometers, and I stopped and said, "Reggie, this is nuts. I'm nuts for listening to you."

"Do you realize we are about to walk into the Cuyahoga County Courthouse and sit down with a judge and talk about protecting a gambling and drug operation?"

I was doing two things. First, I was trying to convince Reggie not to go into the courthouse. And second, I wanted to get this all on tape before they discovered I was wearing a recorder as I passed through the magnetometer. Reggie grabbed my arm and walked me right up to the magnetometer. As we approached the magnetometer, I thought, well, our undercover operation was fun, and it went well, and this was probably not a good way to end it.

But just as we were about to pass through the magnetometer, Reggie pulled me around the side of the magnetometer and told the two court security guards that I was with him. I forgot Reggie spent most of his days there and was friends with just about every security officer there. We walked right in unfettered. Once we passed the security guards and made it past the magnetometer, I think that was when my heart started to beat again. *Phew!* I somehow escaped again!

We met the judge, and she was extremely friendly and cooperative. We actually discussed a plan that we would put in place if one of my guys was caught in Cleveland transporting marijuana. I wasn't sure if this was going to go down, but it was now on the table. Dan and HQ were absolutely ecstatic over this latest development. Now we had to come up with a plan and get FBIHQ and DOJ approval to run this marijuana shipment deal. We could not let this turn into Operation Corkscrew again. We went over the scenario several times. The most important thing was if things weren't going as planned, we would just walk away.

♥ ♥ ♥

August 1990

Reggie introduced me to Lee Wilson, a Cleveland Police Officer who, in turn, introduced me to some of his colleagues at the Cleveland police department that was willing to provide protection for my marijuana filled trucks coming up from Kentucky. On camera, I had six Cleveland Police officers sitting in my office at the warehouse with Reggie telling me how they planned to protect my shipments. They discussed freely what their plan would be and how they would use their police radios and vehicles to get the job done.

The scenario worked like this. Two rental trucks would come to my warehouse at a pre-determined time. One truck they believed to be coming from Kentucky, supposedly carrying a couple of tons of marijuana, would pull into the warehouse. These police officers would be set up around the warehouse to ensure safe arrival.

A second truck coming from somewhere up north Buffalo or the New England area would arrive shortly thereafter and also pull into the warehouse. The two drivers would then exchange vehicles and head back to their previous location. Supposedly the truck heading north had the marijuana and would depart the warehouse first. The police officers would lead and follow that truck until it was safely out of Cuyahoga County. They provided me with a Cleveland PD radio, so I could sit in my office and listen to what was going on. After they had completed their assignment, they would return to my office to brief me on what happened. I would then pay them.

In September 1990, we ran our first marijuana shipment deal, and it went just as planned. Each police officer and Reggie was paid $1500 for their efforts. They really did a great job. They took this very seriously and used every precaution. When they returned to my office, they critiqued their efforts and made some necessary changes that would make the next run even safer.

All of this was caught on video and audio recordings. It was beautiful.

October 1990

I had scheduled another drug shipment. I was sitting in my office waiting for Reggie and his crew of police officers to show up, Dan called.

"You can't do this until we get an okay from the DEA per HQ," Dan ordered.

"Dan, they will be here in less than fifteen minutes. We are doing this."

"No, you can't," he said emphatically. "DEA found out about these drug shipments and contacted FBIHQ. FBIHQ has requested that we coordinate this with the Cleveland DEA. I just put a call into the DEA Office here in Cleveland, I am waiting for their response, and as soon as they let me know, I'll call you."

"Dan, I am telling you right now just, so you know I will not answer the telephone. I will take full responsibility for this. Besides, we have one baggie of marijuana in the truck. We have no alleged drug dealers involved. This is an FBI matter involving corrupt police officers, not a DEA matter. And, I have worked to damn hard to get us where we are on this."

Dan knew I was right and said he understood. Dan was just doing what FBIHQ had ordered him to do. Reggie and his guys showed up at my office, and I unplugged my phone from the wall. As far as I was concerned, it was a go, with or without the approval of the DEA.

"We're here and ready to go," Reggie said. The six cops stood behind him; they were ready.

At 11:00 am sharp, the police officers got in their vehicles and set up around the warehouse. They were informed to take the first truck that exited the building out to Interstate 90 and lead them out of town. The Officers would keep Reggie, and I apprised via Cleveland Police handheld radios that they provided.

After the deal was done and the truck was safely out of Cleveland, the officers returned to my office at the warehouse we went over the operation. We now knew we could pull off this job off without a hitch. The Officers told me that they were willing to do these runs whenever I needed them. I paid the police officers and Reggie $1500 apiece for their efforts, and of course, it was all captured on video, and they left.

I plugged the phone back in. A moment later, it was ringing. It was from Dan. "DEA just let me know they have no problem with us going through with the scenario.

"Great, thank God for the DEA," I said, sarcastically. I then informed Dan that the deal was over and done, and everything went well.

We ran that scenario several more times. Of course, there was no marijuana in the trucks, with the exception of a small plastic baggie that was actually evidence from another case.

I wish we could have gotten Bud and his crew for this. But I would never have attempted this with Bud's team. They were just crazy enough to try and rip me off. However, this group of police officers that Reggie put together was extremely nice, cordial, and always professional. Strange as it sounds, I trusted these guys.

While we were running this drug shipment scenario every other week or so, I was looking for a temporary location to run the casino until I thought it was safe to go back to the warehouse. I was getting pressure from the gamblers and from Reggie to get the casino back up and running.

I found a run-down hotel that had a huge conference room that would work as a make-shift casino, but the logistics were a nightmare. I had to dis-assemble and move the tables from the warehouse to the hotel on Friday afternoon, assemble them, and then dis-assemble them at the end of the night. It was a huge task! On top of that, we could not install cameras or microphones, so we went with a brief-case that housed a video recorder. The hotel was located right next to a local television station, and our tech agents were afraid that our signal may be picked up by the local television stations satellite dishes and could be televised throughout the local viewing area. That would not work well at all! It just was not worth the trouble. Unfortunately, we discovered the video we were getting from the briefcase recorder was not very good. And that would come back to haunt us.

I ran the games at the hotel three more times but decided it just wasn't worth it. Plus, I had additional costs that included renting the hotel and paying the hotel manager and staff to keep quiet. This was really getting on my nerves, and it was starting to show.

I used the guys who protected the marijuana shipments and a few of their colleagues from the Cleveland PD to work security at the hotel. This group included thirteen Cleveland Police officers. We now had twenty-five Cleveland Police Officers on the line for illegal activity.

CHAPTER

26

October 1990

Reggie and his crew were keeping me busy. However, I continued to stay in touch with Shirley, the namesake of SHIRON. Shirley was a great contact and provided me with good advice and intelligence about what was going on within the Cleveland PD. Shirley also continued to send gamblers to my casino, on the weeks I ran it. She was steadfast and always seemed loyal to me. But Dan wanted to test her, to see how honest she really was with me.

Dan and Rick decided to pay Shirley a visit. Shirley was working the bar when Dan and Rick showed up. "You Shirley Carter?" Dan asked.

"Who's asking?" she asked, drying a glass.

He flashed his badge. "I am Dan Estrem from the FBI. FBI in Louisville is looking for Brad Ray Morgan." He said, showing her a picture of me. "He is a big-time drug smuggler and a gambler. You know the guy?"

Shirley put on quite the show. She looked at my picture

and handed it back to Dan. "Sorry, boys. Never heard of him."

"We have done some surveillance and have followed him to your bar on a few occasions," Dan said, trying to put on the pressure.

"Man, this is a titty bar. We get a lot of men through here. I can't possibly remember every Sam, Dick, and Harry that passes through. Can you guys please get out of here? I don't want you scaring away my customers."

Dan and Rick left. Ten minutes later, my phone rang. It was Shirley. "I need you to meet me at 6 pm at Kim's Wings," which was located on St. Clair Avenue, one of the local bars that were famous for their wings.

"I will be there," I said.

I arrived at Shirley's favorite wing place at 5:50. Shirley was already there, seated in the back. I sat down across from her.

"How are you doing, Shirl?" I asked.

"I am good. But I'm not sure I can say the same about you."

"What do you mean?" I asked, knowing full well what she meant.

"Some FBI Agent, Dan Esterball, or something came by my bar today." Dan's name is Estrem, but Shirley called him Dan Esterball. Shirley did not like Dan. I worked hard to hold back the laughter as Shirley butchered Dan's last name, and she did it with great gusto.

"Why?" I asked quizzically.

"He was looking for you. I told him that I didn't know you, but you need to lay low. I will let you know if I hear anything else or if he comes back. But seriously, Ray lay low.

"I will. Thank you, Shirley. I really appreciate it."

"We're friends," she said with a smile.

"Yes, we are,' I replied. *Wow, I was really killing this undercover thing!* We now knew that Shirley trusted me and believed in me. Shirley even tried to protect me.

We ate our dinner and conversed talking shop and gambling. Shirley was an entertaining lady.

I took the check. "I got this," I told her. "I owe you!"

"Thanks, Ray," she paused. As we were headed to our cars, Shirley said, "Can I ask you a favor?"

"Of course," I replied. She asked me to follow her back to her bar.

We had been at the restaurant for almost ninety minutes, and my tape was about to run out. I was going to have to change my tape on the way to Shirley's bar while I was following her. This was not going to be an easy feat.

As we drove off, I began to change the tape in my microcassette recorder that was in my pants. I pulled my zipper down, pulled out the cassette tape that was in the recorder, and put in the new one. No problem.

When we got to Shirley's bar, she parked near the back door, and I parked further down in the parking lot. Shirley motioned for me to go in the back door. As we were walking towards the door, one of her employees exited. She saw both Shirley and I and decided to come over to talk to us. We stood under the only light in the back of the bar, and it cast our shadows onto the parking lot. We stood there for approximately ten minutes when I looked down at our shadows. I saw the shadow of the wire poking out of my zipper.

I had failed to place the recorder in my pants properly, and the wire had slipped down and was now protruding from the zipper of my pants, which I forgot to pull up after changing the tape. I was flabbergasted. I looked at Shirley and her employee to determine if either of them had noticed. If they had seen, they gave no indication as such.

I quickly stated, "I have to go to the men's room," grabbing my crotch and immediately trying to hide the wire. I made it to the bathroom and secured the recorder and the wire. I do not believe either Shirley or her employee knew what had just happened.

Shirley's bar, The Silver Fox, was a strip club that had a dance floor for the girls, several tables around the dance floor, and a large u-shaped bar in the middle of the establishment. There was always loud music. The bar was old had a large parking lot in front and a smaller parking lot for the employees around back. Once inside the Silver Fox, Shirley checked with the bartender and some of her customers and then came back and sat next to me at the bar.

"I am getting married next month," Shirley informed me as proud as she could be.

"That is great, Shirley! Congratulations." I said.

"Thanks! And I am excited, but I don't have much family to speak of. I was wondering if you would do me the honor of giving me away at my wedding."

"I would be honored!" I said.

Shirley gave me details about the wedding. She was so excited and happy. I was willing to give her away. But now, I'm thinking to myself. I'll probably need to get FBIHQ's approval to do this. Hopefully, they would say yes, because I planned on giving Shirley away at her wedding no matter what. I figured getting FBIHQ approval was Dan's problem. The next day I played the tape for Dan, where Shirley asked me to give her away at her wedding. Dan just laughed, shook his head, and said I'll see what I can do.

November 1990

Shirley got married, and I proudly gave her away. We had a lovely little reception that included the cake and champagne for the bride, groom, their family members, and a few friends. Shirley and her new husband thanked me. A few months from now, they would not be thinking so highly of me. But for now, I'd enjoy the moment. I know Shirley truly enjoyed all of it at the time. But later, when she was arrested and learned of my true identity, she was absolutely furious. And when I had to positively identify her, she spat at me. I am sure after that, whenever she would look at her wedding photos and see me, she would probably just scream.

We eventually made it back to the east side warehouse and were up and running just like before. I felt much more at ease with this group of police officers than I ever did with Bud and his group. The crowds were getting bigger, and once again, it was getting tight even though this space was much bigger than the one on the west side. Also, all the GM auto parts were getting a lot of attention, and I had many offers to buy some or all, which I had to continually turned down.

Bud was now officially out, and Reggie's crew now had all my focus. I kept waiting to hear from Bud but never did. During this period of the operation, Dan had made the determination that he needed additional agents to start reviewing, transcribing and marking the tape recordings, both video, and audio, for evidence. Dan did not want to wait until after the operation was finished to do this as he wanted the trials to begin as soon as possible, and the only way to accomplish that was by starting the review process now.

In order for this to work, they had to ensure that with every recording, whether it was audio or video and whoever was on the tape (i.e., subjects) and copies of those tapes would be needed for discovery purposes. So, if there were fifteen subjects on a particular video recording, then each subject would eventually require a copy of the tape for trial purposes. This was an enormous undertaking that required an entire squad of agents. They also had to transcribe the audio portion of the tape, which would require the same amount of work as far as copies for each subject overheard on the audio recording.

Dan and his squad of agents worked to complete these prosecutive materials and get them ready for trial. This would ensure there would be a little delay for the start of the trials, which would begin almost immediately after the arrests were effected.

In order to keep this huge undertaking completely confidential, this squad of agents was secluded from the rest of the Cleveland FBI, and only those assigned to this case were authorized to enter this area. This also kept word from spreading to the local task force officers who were assigned to work in the Cleveland FBI office. To demonstrate just how well this secret was kept among only those agents on Dan's squad when the arrests were made, the entire office was in shock.

CHAPTER

SHIRON the fourth six months

In December 1990, SHIRON was approved for another six months. We had hoped that this would be our opportunity to go after some judges and possibly even some other public officials Reggie had identified. We were ready to go. Everything was in place, and then Reggie called from jail. He had been arrested. I attempted to re-contact the judges that Reggie had introduced me to as well as some other public officials, but no one would talk. Reggie became kryptonite. All of Reggie's contacts were afraid he might be cooperating as he was facing some lengthy jail time. They wanted no part of anything that we had discussed. It wasn't me; they did not trust it was Reggie.

After another month, Dan and I decided that although we could have continued to run the casino and bring in even more police officers, but we had made our point.

Consequently, it was decided that the last six months, I would only run a few more games as I had some additional police officers, I had promised I would bring on board.

I had spent the past year and a half living and socializing with people I could not stand to be around. I was tired of living this lie and wanted this thing to end. At this point, my undercover operation had netted more police officers than almost any other police corruption investigation in the history of the FBI. Everyone was satisfied. We could have continued, but everyone on my team was tired. Everyone from Dan, Rick, Herb, and the FBI Cleveland's front office to the agents assigned to listen and transcribe all my tape recordings, the USAO, was all ready to close this down.

We ran the casino for a few more months. Then on March 15, 1991, we shut it down. We added five more police officers bringing our total to 30 Cleveland Police Officers. We ended up arresting 17 other individuals for drugs, stolen property, bookmaking, etc.

April 1991

Although we were done running games and I had closed the casino, I still maintained a low profile for the next two months. I continued to run the Tee-Shirt shop and began getting rid of all of the gambling equipment and my inventory at the shop.

As we started the final stages of the indictments, Dan brought in the Behavioral Science Unit from Quantico. This unit provides assistance to all law enforcement agencies via the use of criminal investigative analysis. This process was developed by reviewing crimes or illegal activity from both a behavioral and investigative perspective. Their process involves reviewing and assessing the facts of the criminal acts involving the subject(s) of an investigation.

They interpret the subjects' behavior and their interactions with others involved. This unit conducts a detailed analysis of the crimes to assist with a myriad of investigative actions, one being interview strategies.

After the Behavioral Science Unit had time to analyze our subjects, they called Dan and me in for a meeting. They sat down and reviewed the video and audiotapes of all the police officers involved. The Behavioral Science psychologists would meet with Dan and me periodically to ask questions about individual police officers. They had decided on the best target and best approach for taking down the officers and perhaps gaining additional information on corruption within the hierarchy of the PD.

They agreed that the best approach was to develop a 'Flip' scenario. They had analyzed the behaviors of all of the police subjects determined which police officer would be the most willing to cooperate with the investigation. They picked someone they felt that could provide us with pertinent information on high ranking officials within the Cleveland Police Department and would be willing to spill the beans on what they knew about any corruption. They based their decisions on behaviors and personality from their tedious and thorough research they had conducted. After several weeks of watching and listening intently to the hundreds of video and audiotapes, they decided upon Martin Shaw.

Dan and I didn't agree with their choice but had to go

along as this was their assessment. It was decided if this scenario worked, we would put off the arrests and attempt to approach higher-level management within the Cleveland Police Department. We all decided it would definitely be worth our time if we were able to identify corruption among the higher-ranking police officers within the department. I was certainly willing to give it a go.

Once a subject is identified, the Flip scenario is designed to develop a scenario to get that subject to cooperate. This involved days of surveillance on Martin Shaw. They learned everything they could about his family, about his beliefs, his desires, everything that meant anything to this officer they studied it.

Once they had that information, they wrote a script tailored to affect him and subsequently make him talk. The script was for SAC Branon to read and memorize for when they brought this officer in. SAC Branon was instructed on what to say, when to say and how to say it.

They also set up various phases where the subject would be subjected to brief periods of sensory overload with information and what appeared to be evidence.

They set the day and time the Flip was to take place. The FBI would follow Martin Shaw and, at a predetermined location, pull him over and place him in an FBI vehicle. The FBI agents that would pick him up and escort him to the Cleveland FBI office were provided a script by the Behavioral Science guys as to precisely what they were to say to the officer and nothing more. All they would say was that the SAC wanted to speak with him.

Everything went as planned, and SAC Branon did a masterful job as he perfectly executed his pitch. The officer agreed to cooperate but wanted to be allowed to go home to recover from all of this and come back the next day as he stated he was completely overwhelmed. They let him go home, and he came back the next day.

When he returned the next day, Mr. Shaw was completely out of his mind. He rambled as he spoke and wasn't making any sense. Those that witnessed this stated they believed he was absolutely trying to cooperate, but it appeared that he had lost his mind. They got what they could, then decided to let him go back home, get some rest, and they would talk to him in a few days. He never fully recovered and could not provide any useful information. We really did not need his information unless he had something on higher-ranking officers. He never offered that type of information. He pleaded guilty, and just prior to his sentencing, he killed himself.

As the operation was winding down, I started to go home more. I was starting to mend my relationship with my family. This was now my main priority. I began to inquire if I could be transferred to Youngstown, Ohio. It was only thirty minutes from Pittsburgh and was extremely reasonable as far as the cost of living. My SAC Bill Brannon said that he was under the impression that FBIHQ has agreed to allow me to be transferred to the Youngstown Resident Agency. This made sense as I would only be about 75 miles from Cleveland and could commute back and forth each day as we prepared for the trials. And I could be with my family. Be normal once again.

However, as the undercover operation was winding down, FBIHQ asked the Cleveland FBI office to conduct a threat assessment. In other words, would my family or I be in danger of retaliation because of my role in the operation. Unbeknownst to me, this was being done. We were close to shutting everything down when I got a page to call Dan. I called him back right away.

"Bad news Ray," he said, "The result of the assessment showed that there is a real possibility that either you or your family could be seriously at risk staying near Cleveland. Based on that, FBIHQ has changed its mind and will not approve your transfer to Youngstown."

"Where do they want me to go?"

"They gave you three options, New York, Detroit, or Newark."

I guess the old adage was true, "in the FBI no good deed goes unpunished." I was furious and began yelling at Dan, which was absolutely the wrong thing to do as Dan had worked hard to get everyone to agree to send me to Youngstown. But who else was I going to yell at?

Dan listened as I vented and then asked, "Is there somewhere else you would like to go? FBIHQ just thinks Youngstown is too close."

Two years of my life, numerous sacrifices, and I just wanted to go to Youngstown, Ohio. How many people say just send me to Youngstown, OH and I'll be happy? Not many! But that wasn't going to be an option. So, I had to come up with somewhere. "How about Pittsburgh?"

"I will see what they say," Dan said.

I heard back from Dan the next day. "FBIHQ said no to Pittsburgh as you still have to do your top twelve. But they will let you pick which of the top twelve offices you would like to go to. But they have added three cities to the list Dallas, Atlanta, and Houston, and you can choose one of those if you like."

I was angry. I had just completed two years of pure hell. I had just sacrificed two years of being away from my family. The time I would never get back. I had made one of the most significant police corruption cases in the history of the FBI, and this is the best they can do.

"I will think about it," I told Dan.

"You only have a few days to decide," he reminded me.

I drove back to Pittsburgh to discuss it with Lynn. She was far from happy, and we went in circles going over the options. Finally, we decided Atlanta would be the best. Low cost of living decent weather and the fact that she had been working for Delta, she would probably be able to continue since Atlanta was their central hub. If this was the best the FBI could offer, then Atlanta would be the best place for us.

As we got closer to bringing SHIRON to a close, it was time to bring Edward Kovacic, the Chief of the Cleveland Police Department in to brief him on our investigation. Chief Kovacic was not happy that we did not bring him and his department in from the beginning, but Dan and the FBI front office explained why they didn't. And although he was not pleased, he begrudgingly understood and expressed his appreciation for what we had done.

We brought Chief Kovacic in so he would not be embarrassed by the investigation. At the press conference after the arrests, our SAC Bill Brannon stated that the Cleveland Police Department was our partner throughout the investigation and provided valuable assistance. This wasn't true. However, we needed to say this so Cleveland PD could save face and not to further tarnish their reputation, which was about to take a beating from the media and the public.

May 1991

Now it was time to make the arrests. There were several large meetings between the FBI and the Cleveland Police Department. This was going to be extremely dangerous, and the media was going to be all over this. The arrest planning was meticulous by the FBI. The logistics of an arrest raid, and the plan was flawless. FBI Agents from all over Ohio and other neighboring FBI offices were brought in to help with the arrests.

There was a tremendous amount of logistical work that needed to be accomplished. The fact that they would be arresting armed police officers made it even more difficult. Plans were made to minimize this as much as possible, but nevertheless, we still wanted at least three FBI agents per arrestee.

The next day, the arrests were made without any issues or incidents. I had to be at the FBI Office, where the subjects were brought to be fingerprinted and photographed. The arresting agents would have to bring their arrestee to me, so I could positively identify the individual as being the correct person. Several of the arrested officers, when brought to me, did not even acknowledge me. One of the police officers that was arrested was the police officer of the year in Cleveland just a few years prior.

A few of the arrestees, when brought to me, told me not to say anything they would get me a good lawyer. They still did not believe I was an FBI Agent. A few made some serious threats right to my face. Shirley spat at me and yelled out every vulgarity she could think of. But it didn't matter; I was done. I could head home to my family. Every major newspaper in the country had this story. It was even on the front page of USA Today.

There was a mass amount of manpower utilized during this undercover operation. At the conclusion of the investigation, there had been approximately fifteen agents that had been assigned a specific UC role or support role in the case. During the takedown, there were even more agents utilized for the arrests and processing.

There were also agents assigned to surveillance teams, monitoring the numerous Title III's that Dan wrote. There were agents assisting in trial preparation. They were involved in reviewing tapes, transcripts, and videos, office staff providing support in the office typing, filing, and helping with finances. What was unique was that almost everybody assigned to provide administrative support, agents or non-agents, worked extremely well together, and as a result, very shortly after the arrests, massive amounts of evidence were made ready for the defendant's attorneys, and the trials began almost immediately. This was unheard of on a case of this magnitude; usually, prosecution prep took a year or more.

Forty-seven people indicted and arrested. Not bad.

At the end of a very long day, I was extremely proud to

be a part of this team and to have had the opportunity to work with Dan, Rick Herb, and Bob. This undercover operation was a success because of the work and dedication of so many. Now I was ready to get back to my family and a healthier life.

As soon as I was done identifying the last of the arrestees, I said my good-byes to Dan, Rick, Herb, Bob and Mr. Branon got in my car drove back to Hopewell.

My first stop was to the church I used to attend when I was growing up, and I met with Father O'Connell, my childhood priest. I had not seen Father O'Connell for quite some time. But I felt it was essential to get absolution for those past two years. Father O'Connell and I spoke for almost two hours.

I felt much better when we were finished, and I believe that truly helped me move on. I learned a lot from the experience and a lot about myself. It takes a different breed of individual to do something like that, and I have developed the deepest of respect for those who do it the right way for the right reasons.

I cannot express my gratitude to the excellent team that worked with me. They meant so much to me during the operation, but they really have no idea how significant a role they played in keeping me sane. The trust and confidence they displayed in a very young and inexperienced agent is something I will never forget. Dan Estrem was the best-case agent I ever worked with. His dogged determination, and ability to always stay way ahead of everyone else was amazing. Dan was instrumental in never letting all of the administrative bullshit that went on during the operation get to me. And for that, I am forever grateful. With all that being said, the most essential thing in Dan's life was his family. And I admired that.

Rick Hoke was the quintessential FBI Special Agent. Rick was always professional and courteous, and his love for the FBI was more than admirable. But like Dan, Rick's family was of the utmost importance to him. And later in my career, when I was named the Special Agent in Charge of the Pittsburgh FBI Field Office, one of my agents was Matthew Hoke, Rick's son. What an honor that was for me. In some of our conversations during the operation, Rick would talk about Matthew and his family to take my mind off the operation, and I always appreciated those conversations.

Herb Cohrs was the most exceptional supervisor I have ever worked for. Herb was brilliant and knowledgeable, but more importantly, Herb was very personable as well. He always made me feel important and was SHIRON's biggest supporter.

Robert "Bob" Bulford was without exception the best Assistant United States Attorney I ever worked with. Bob was aggressive and took chances that most AUSAs wouldn't. Bob possessed a great sense of humor and a pleasant personality. And he, along with Joe Schmidt, (who joined our team as we prepared for the trial) were a great team. Bob, the aggressive one, Joe more methodical and cerebral. I loved working with both of them as I spent a significant amount of time with both of them as we spent most of 1992 preparing and going to trial.

There were so many others, too many to thank individually, who played an essential role in putting this all together and I am in awe of all of them,

SHIRON *Aftermath*

For me, the case was over except for the trial preparation and the trials. For Dan, it was another headache as he had to, as he has said many times babysit the AUSAs in trial prep, dispose of property, closeout books all while he was working on new cases he had initiated. There were also real estate issues to deal with, furniture to dispose of, and a significant amount of technical equipment to take care of. In addition, as part of the trial preparation, Dan had video-tapes reproduced as they were made rather than waiting for the end of the case. Dan realized that this would speed the trial process along.

Every defendant had to have a copy of every tape they were recorded on, which meant that dozens of tapes had to be reproduced from each event that was held involving someone who could be prosecuted. At one point, there was a bank of VCR recorders about 30 or so going almost 24 hours a day.

While Dan was busy prepping for trial, the FBI covertly moved my family, and any inquiry concerning our where-abouts went directly to FBIHQ. The FBI made arrangements to sell our house, which they took our names off of any documents related to the house. They packed up all our belongings, sent them to our new place in Atlanta, and re-moved our names from everything. As far as anyone outside the FBI knew, we no longer existed.

In the meantime, I was sent to the FBI Academy at the end of the operation for a couple of weeks to take my final psychological tests, unwind and sit in on whatever classes I wanted to sit in on and to work on my firearms skills once more as it had been more than two years since I had fired my weapon.

I had just finished my psychological tests and was sitting in the lounge area near the cafeteria when one of my former instructors, walked by and saw me sitting there. He was one of my favorite instructors. He had taught communications, both oral and written, FBI communications. I loved his class.

He asked me what I was doing, at the academy and I explained to him why I was there. He was ecstatic to hear what I had done and asked if I would be willing to talk to his class. He told me he wanted his class to hear for themselves about the opportunities that are available to first office agents. He said for some reason, this class thinks they will only be doing background investigations. I said I would be happy to and he told me the room number and to be there at 2:00 pm.

I had not prepared anything but thought I could easily talk about this to first office agents. I ate lunch, and then just prior to 2:00 pm I walked into his class and sat in the back of the room. He stopped and gave his class a ten-minute break and informed them that he had a guest speaker for the last hour. When the class broke, I went up to the front of the class and was talking to the instructor with my back to the students.

After they all had returned and were seated, I turned around and looked at the class as he introduced me. As I looked around the classroom, I noticed an older looking man, someone I thought to be in his fifties. I thought, what is this person doing in class he looks like he could be retired? But he had on the uniform khaki slacks and the FBI polo shirt. I looked one more time at the older man. And then I realized, it was Joe Pistone, the real-life Donnie Brasco was attending my talk!

I had previously heard that Joe got fed up with FBI management after his undercover operation and all the trials that followed. I had heard he quit, but never knew why. However, I was unaware that he had come back.

Now here I was, talking about undercover work with the FBI's Godfather of the undercover program sitting in the audience. I spoke to the class for an hour, and I mentioned the book Donnie Brasco several times. I never indicated that he was sitting in the classroom, and if anyone in the class knew no one let on.

At the end, I received a standing ovation from the class, including Joe. Several of the students stopped to congratulate me and asked a few questions. Then Joe walked by me, brushed my arm, and said, "Nice job, kid!"

Joe Pistone just said to me, "Nice job, kid." I was walking on air when I left the classroom. About fifteen minutes later, I hear my name over the loudspeaker, and I was told to report to the Assistant Director's ("ADs") office. I had no clue why I had to go to the AD's office other than there might be a problem at home. When I walked in, I was greeted by AD Tony Daniels who welcomed me into his office. And sitting on a chair in his office was Joe Pistone.

"Mr. Pistone would like to meet you," AD Daniels said to me.

I almost fell over *Joe Pistone wants to meet me?* Joe, Mr. Daniels, and I talked for over an hour. I thought I had died and gone to undercover heaven. I learned during our conversation that Mr. Daniels was one of Joe's supervisors during his undercover days. My entire two years were spent emulating and referencing Joe Pistone, and now here I was, with him, receiving accolades. I knew right then that everything I had done all the sacrifices I had made had been well worth it.

● ● ●

Although I had been assigned to the Atlanta Division, I really did not spend much time there as I continuously traveled to Cleveland to prepare for the trials. I was once again leaving my family all week. I felt terrible. But knowing we were finally close to the end of the tunnel. I could see the light.

The trial preparations were going exceptionally well. But inevitably, all of the defendants were starting to plead guilty. So, as we got ready for the first trial, only one defendant of that first group remained. And he just happened to be a former Cleveland Police Officer of the Year.

The trial began. I was on the stand for four consecutive days on direct and two more days on cross-examination. Bob was well prepared, and Bob started my direct examination, and for four days, I answered all of Bob's questions. Most of the evidence was also introduced through me. All of the pertinent video and audio recordings, the FBI 302s that I authored (FBI 302s are our investigative reports), transcripts, photos whatever we had that was relevant to our case.

I breezed through the direct examination, and then after four days, the cross-examination from the defense attorney was next. The defense attorney started right off the bat by referring to our undercover operation as a "sting." And every time he used the word sting, I responded with I have no idea what a sting is. He did not like that response but continued down that path, and every time he used the word sting, I provided my answer, "I have no idea what a sting is."

I even explained that in the FBI Investigative manuals, we have undercover operations, and there are different types of undercover operations, but nowhere in our manual do we identify these types of investigations as a sting. Finally, after numerous attempts by the defense attorney to get me to respond to that line of questioning, the judge stopped him and said, "I believe the witness has addressed that on several occasions in the FBI there is no such thing as a sting operation."

His next move was to discredit me by calling me a liar constantly. He stated that I lied to his client about who I really was. He tried to question my credibility over and over. He worked hard to get something to stick to discredit me in order to defend his client.

After I testified, I was not permitted back in the courtroom to watch or listen to any of the other witnesses in case I had to be called back for rebuttal. When it came to the closing arguments, I was in the front row of the gallery right behind the prosecution table. I did not want to miss this. The defense attorney started his closing arguments with: "The prosecution's main witness is a liar." All the while, he is making his way back to near where I was sitting in the gallery. He finished by turning to me, placed his hands on the rail, and said, "Shame on you agent Morrow, shame on you."

I knew that was a good sign for us as he had nothing to defend his client with, he could only attempt to attack me and my credibility. It just did not work.

The next day the Cleveland Plain Dealer newspaper's

RAY A. MORROW WITH LINDSAY PRESTON

headline read, "FBI Agent Lied." The article explained in detail that I was merely accused of lying by the defense attorney, not that I actually lied. I had to read that part to my mother several times before she believed me.

The next day the headlines read, "Cleveland Police Officer found guilty." The first trial was over. It was a great feeling to get that first one out of the way and get ready for the second group.

♥ ♥ ♥

April 1993

I was still traveling most of the time. But my life was getting back on track. We were even expecting our third child. And on Tuesday, April 20, 1993, my daughter Taylor was born. Lynn and I were elated. We had three healthy, happy children, and the last of the trials were wrapping up.

All of the defendants in the second trial all pled guilty. All that prep work and no trials. That just confirmed our beliefs that our investigation was impeccable. Yet we still had one more to go.

Again, all but one of the police officers from the last group, plead guilty. This one would be difficult as this police officer only worked for me twice, and that was at the hotel where we only had one camera, and that was in a briefcase. The quality of the video from the briefcase camera was not very good, and several times the briefcase had been inadvertently moved. This created a huge problem in that it was moved, and placed upright, causing the camera to video the ceiling for large parts of the evening until one of us agents realized and then moved it back into place.

This trial did not go as well as the first. The prosecutors did another great job, and I was not on the stand for more than two days total. The issue that came up was the police officer claimed he was too drunk and did not know what he was doing. I have to admit he was drunk, and when he was on camera, you could easily see he was inebriated. He was found not guilty. We were all pretty upset that the jury accepted that excuse. But we were done. And I was off to Atlanta for good. You can't win them all.

Two years later, I got a call from Joe Pistone. At the time, I was the White-Collar Crimes Supervisor of the FBI's Tampa Division. Joe asked if I would join him, and Steve Salmieri (Steve was the first FBI undercover agent to go undercover in federal prison) in Budapest, Hungary, at the International Law Enforcement Academy to teach undercover to the former Soviet bloc countries; Russia, Poland, Romania, Hungary, etc. This had never been done before. The FBI teaching these former soviet bloc countries undercover was unprecedented. It was such an honor to be asked by Joe Pistone to participate in such a historical event.

I often look back to my childhood, to the days when I used to watch Inspector Erskine quickly solve cases for the FBI. The FBI was everything I wanted and more. And while my time with the FBI was far from an open and shut case, I loved every minute and I am extremely proud to say I was a Special Agent with the FBI.

My father was unequivocally correct when he told me, "If you love what you do, you'll never have to work a day in your life." And I loved being a Special Agent for the FBI.

I followed my dream to be Inspector Erskine, and it turned out to be an even more fantastic journey than I could have imagined.

ACKNOWLEDGMENTS

I never intended to write a book about my experience. But after much thought and consideration, I decided to do so. It is with great enthusiasm that I acknowledge several people who were instrumental in my writing this book. I rarely, if ever, talked about my time in the FBI and especially about the undercover operation. I was delighted that the operation was successful and that my family and I together were able to move on. I was fortunate enough to move up through the FBI executive management ranks ending my career as the Special Agent in Charge of the Pittsburgh Field Office. My hometown, what an honor and privilege that was, and I wore that honor proudly. No one will ever know how significant an event that was for me.

So, for more than twenty-two years, my undercover story stayed with me. I shared it with no one. My wife, Lynn, never asked, nor did any of my children; they just knew I did not talk about it. It wasn't until I started with the PA Turnpike Commission ("PTC") in January 2014, there were several stories written about my career and my joining the PTC in the local news. A few months later, I received a call from a gentleman who owned a company that had done business with the PTC in the past and wanted to speak with me regarding some pertinent information that he wanted to pass along to the PTC.

At the meeting, this gentleman mentioned some of the articles that he had read about me and started to inquire about my time in the FBI. I had mentioned the undercover operation, and that seemed to really pique his interest. About one hour later, I suggested that we talk about what he had called me about. At the end of our conversation, he asked me if my children were aware of my undercover operation, and I responded that, for the most part, they were not. He suggested that I take the time to write something to them that would memorialize what I had accomplished. He said, "they would be astonished and proud of what their father had accomplished. On my three-hour drive back to Harrisburg, PA, I thought long and hard about what the gentleman had suggested and decided that I would. I went home that weekend and wrote a seventy-three-page letter to my wife and children detailing my undercover operation experience.

In October 2018, I was asked to do a podcast with Ms. Jerri Williams, a retired FBI Special Agent who had written two books and had been using her podcast to bring closed very significant some even historical FBI cases to the public by interviewing the case agents. Jerri has done a great service to the FBI and to the agents who worked these investigations and until now had not been shared so publicly. Ms. Williams asked prior to our podcast if I had written anything to document the investigation, and I mentioned the letter I wrote to my children. She asked if I would send that to her so she could get a better understanding of the case.

After reading my letter, she suggested that I write a book. I laughed at the suggestion, but Jerri was quite serious and again suggested that I consider it. I did the podcast along with Dan Estrem. Dan, after much begging and cajoling on my part, agreed to do the podcast.

After the podcast, I received a call from Joaquin "Jack" Garcia, a retired FBI agent who was renowned for his undercover exploits, infiltrating the Gambino crime family, which were legendary. I had never met Jack but knew of him. Jack had been on "Sixty Minutes" regarding his undercover life and had written a book titled. "Making Jack Falcone: An Undercover FBI Agent Takes Down a Mafia Family." A great read, I might add.

Jack stated that he had heard my podcast and was impressed with my story. Jack suggested I write a book about my undercover experience. So here I have two FBI agents and accomplished authors suggesting that I write a book. I started to consider writing a book seriously, but I wanted to check with one more individual. I called Joe Pistone, and Joe wholeheartedly agreed. So, with the backing and encouragement of Jerri Williams, Jack Garcia, Joe Pistone, and my daughter Taylor, I started the process.

Through Joe Pistone's help, I was able to convince Literary Agent, Mr. Robert Diforio, to take me on as a client. With that, Mr. Diforio put me in touch with one of his editors Ms. Lindsay Friedman. Ms. Friedman made this journey an exciting learning experience. Ms. Friedman was an absolute pleasure to work with. So, to Jerri, Jack, Joe, Robert, Taylor, and Lindsay, I want to say thank you for having the confidence in me and providing the support and guidance I needed to bring this to fruition.

The FBI is a cradle for talented, intelligent, driven, and dedicated employees. The range of diversity, experience, and wisdom is beyond comprehension. In my mind, they are the best of the best. Throughout my FBI career, I had the opportunity and pleasure to work with some exceptionally talented individuals who were exemplary examples of what an FBI employee should be. And at each stop throughout my career, I had the good fortune to meet and work with some of the best the FBI had to offer. Individuals who made a lasting impression on me and helped shape not only my career but also my leadership style.

One of my greatest FBI honors I had was being assigned to the FBI Director's Protection Detail with FBI Director Louis J. Freeh. Director Freeh was absolutely one of the greatest leaders I ever had the opportunity to work with. Director Freeh was a brilliant administrator, who possessed an engaging and caring personality. A true family man who never let his duties or responsibilities interfere with his family activities. I truly admired the way he carried himself and how well he treated all he came in contact with. He would always acknowledge and graciously thank those that assisted in his protection detail. Director Freeh was simply a class act. And I am a much better person for having had the opportunity of working with him.

When I was assigned to the FBI Director's Protective Detail, I worked closely with a close-knit group of agents all of the same mindset. Protect the Director and the integrity of the FBI at all costs. Our supervisor was Mark Babyak, a solid, quietly effective leader who provided outstanding guidance and support. I learned from the more senior agents on the detail like Fred Snellings, Frank Battle and

Tom Almon who were on the detail prior to my arrival and they took the other newly assigned agents and me under their wing, The group I came in with was a special group, and they included, Walt Reynolds and Icey Jenkins. John Griglione, one of the drivers who was also deputized as a U.S. marshal and was, therefore, qualified to carry a firearm and when Director Freeh made the decision to eliminate his security detail, John became not only his driver but also his security detail. John was an outstanding employee and became a trusted friend of mine. I was confident that when the Director eliminated his detail, he was still in good hands with John.

I quickly determined that Director Freeh had surrounded himself with some high-quality people who served him well throughout his tenure. Bob Bucknam, Director Freeh's Chief of Staff, Jim Bucknam, Senior Advisor, Howard Shapiro, General Counsel, were all particularly proficient in their roles, and I found them remarkable. John Behnke, a Special Assistant to the Director, was an extraordinarily competent special agent, one that Director Freeh often described as "without exception the very best FBI investigator he had ever met. To this day, I have the utmost respect for all of these gentlemen.

I left the Director's Detail and was assigned as a supervisor in the Undercover and Sensitive Operations Unit ("USOU"). Here I met and worked with the Unit Chief Vince Wincelowicz, who not only served as a mentor to me when I was undercover but also provided great insights into the undercover arena from his vast undercover experiences. Ms. Ronnie Bobbitt was a support employee who took great pride in her role and provided the necessary guidance and support to help me through the never-ending administrative stuff that went along with the assignment. I also had the opportunity to work with Steve Salmieri, another FBI Undercover all-star.

There are a few others who had a substantial and most positive impact on my career. In Tampa, my first field supervisory position, Pete Wubbenhorst, the Tampa Division's Chief Counsel. Larry Albert, Assistant Special Agent in Charge, James "Chip" Burrus, Supervisor, Orlando Resident Agency, Eddie Tuttle, John Mule, Dean Schmidt, and Sue Bucenell all agents assigned to my White-Collar Crime Squad.

In the Minneapolis Division, where I served as the Assistant Special Agent in Charge, Rick Ostrom, Supervisor White-Collar Crime Squad, Ronna Trog, my very effective and efficient Executive Administrative Assistant and once again James "Chip" Burrus who convinced me to consider applying for the Assistant Special Agent in Charge of the Minneapolis Division.

At the Criminal Justice Information Services Division ("CJIS"), Tom Bush, Steve Fischer, and Sheila Hartley Fischer. And in the New York Field Office, where I served as the Special Agent in Charge of the Administration Division. The division, I spent the early part of my career avoiding and found that it was a wonderful place to work and absolutely amazing people there to do the work. Andy Arena, Special Agent in Charge of the Criminal Division and Donald J. Ackerman, Assistant Special Agent in Charge, Criminal Division, were my go-to guys whenever I needed to get the pulse of the office. There were so many others in the New Your Field Office that just impressed the hell out of me, far too many to name here. I'll just say the people of the New York Field Office amazed me.

In Pittsburgh, where I served as the Special Agent in Charge, my two Assistant Special Agents in Charge, Bob Rudge, and Kevin Deegan, two of the best I ever served with, along with Jeff Killeen Chief Division Counsel, Ed Daer my SWAT Team leader and Quantico class mate and again so many others who made this office special.

I would be remiss if I did not thank my lovely wife of 41 years, Lynn and my three children, Ross, Blake, and Taylor, who are all grown up and living very productive and fruitful lives. I am so proud of them. Without them, none of this possible, and for that, I am forever grateful.

ABOUT THE AUTHORS

Ray A. Morrow served as the primary FBI undercover agent in a major police corruption investigation that netted thirty Cleveland Police. As a first time author of Broken Shield: An FBI Undercover Agent's Personal Perspective, he provides details both professionally and personally of the highs and lows he encountered during his time undercover.

Ray is an accomplished leader in the FBI, having served as the Special Agent in Charge of both the New York and Pittsburgh Field Offices. Ray possesses an all-encompassing background in investigative field operations combined with high-caliber qualifications in executive investigative management. Ray also protected two FBI Directors, the President of a Fortune 500 Company as well as the President of the United States as a member of the U.S. Secret Service Uniformed Division. Ray now serves as the Chief Compliance Officer for the Pennsylvania Turnpike Commission. His more than forty-three years of investigations, executive management and executive protection highlight his undercover journey. Ray waited twenty-eight years to tell his story, a story even his wife and children never truly knew.

Lindsay Preston has written numerous nonfiction works for some of the most prominent figures in the business, law enforcement and sports. She is the creator of Writingroom. com, forging a community for aspiring writers. She lives in the Cleveland, Ohio with her young daughter.

.